Insects

&

Icebergs

A Memoir of Sorts
featuring
Poems for Children
and Selected Adults

Insects
&
Icebergs

A Memoir of Sorts
featuring
Poems for Children
and Selected Adults

 Stanton Klose

SUKKELA POIKA PRODUCTIONS

Insects & Icebergs

Most names have been changed to respect privacy.

Publisher: SUKKELA POIKA PRODUCTIONS

ISBN 978-1-7327747-5-9

Edited by: Laurie McAndish King
Cover Photo: 123RF stock
Book Design: Jim Shubin, BookAlchemist.net

For my families on Prospect Street,
Ho'okeha Street and Autumn Lane

Thank You
Book Passage, Cyra McFadden, Laurie King,
Jim Shubin and the More Than
a Mystery Writers' Group: Cynthia, Frances,
Jill, Nicola and Vicki

Who's Who

My Father: Orval M Klose. (There is no period after the M, which served as his middle name.) Born 1913 in Napa, California. Died 1975 in Arcata, California. He was an able seaman in the Merchant Marine during the 1930s, and a navigator with the Army Air Force Air Transport Command during World War II. He earned a BA from the University of California at Berkeley, an MA from the University of Chicago, and a PhD from the University of Washington. He taught mathematics at Seattle University and Humboldt State University.

My Mother: Rachel Elami Klose, nee Nurmi. Born 1915 in Sortavala, Finland. Died 2000 in Arcata, California. Married to Gordon Blackwell, then to my father.

My Older Sister: Judith Karen Flores, nee Blackwell. Born 1940 in Seattle, Washington. She attended the University of Washington, then moved to Honolulu in 1962. Married with one son, Christopher Moke Kuhilani Flores, and three grandsons. She worked for many years in the airline industry, and is now retired on Oahu.

My Younger Sister: Kathleen Rae Klose. Born 1950 in Seattle, Washington. She has BAs in French-Linguistics and Computer Science from the University of California at Santa Cruz. Married with one daughter, Rachel Ilana Harris. She lives in Massachusetts, where she teaches English to adult immigrants.

Me: Patrick Stanton Klose. Born 1949 in Seattle, Washington. I have an AB in Environmental Studies and an MA in Architecture from the University of California at Berkeley. I worked for thirty-six years as an environmental graphic designer/project manager. I am now retired in Northern California.

Toy Stories I:
Construction Projects

CHILDHOOD CAN BE FRUSTRATING if you think of yourself as a particularly small adult. You watch the full-size ones act with maddening competence and you cannot mimic them. They can draw a cat that looks like a cat. You cannot. They can write their names—and yours—in legible letters neatly arrayed. You cannot, and neither can you cut your meat safely nor coax your shoelaces into matching loops. Then you discover Lincoln Logs, and suddenly you, too, can have agency in the world.

In retrospect, I rate Lincoln Logs right up there with learning to *carry the 1*. Lincoln Logs were mistake-proof. All the long logs were precisely the same length, and so were all the mediums and the shorts. The notches at each end of every log were cut to the same tight tolerance. My younger sister, Kath, and I periodically dumped our can of Lincoln Logs onto the floor and then stacked and interlocked and stacked until we'd assembled a cabin so true and plumb that Lincoln himself would have smiled gravely and nodded.

If Lincoln Logs had a failing, it was that you could only build three or four different cabins with them. They were like that jigsaw puzzle with the two ducklings cuddled together in a grass-lined nest. Adorable, those ducklings, but once you could fit the eight pieces together in the dark, it was time to move on.

Kath and I moved on to Block City, and here our parents had been uncharacteristically generous. They bought us the Chicagoan set, which included 310 blocks, sixty-five half blocks, six doors and fifteen windows that we could share nicely. Block City blocks were like LEGOs, but white and smaller—about an inch long and half an inch wide and high. The doors and windows were red. Based on the illustrations on the round cardboard can the blocks came in, we could build the San Fernando, the Hollywood or the Malibou [sic] Beach, but we preferred to serve as our own architects. Sometimes we built custom homes, but more often we built towers or zigzagging walls.

It was fundamentally satisfying to work as a Block City mason, assembling a wall block by block, row above row. There was a friendly click as each block fit into the two blocks beneath it to become part of an overlapping pattern as old as the Great Pyramids.

Kath and I would sometimes leave one of our completed structures intact for a while so we could admire it, but demolition was, to be honest, more fun than construction. Pulling a block off a wall was a little like wiggling a loose tooth, and we pulled and pulled until we'd piled up a heap that looked like the aftermath of a South American earthquake.

We had a big can of Tinkertoys, too. Like the Block City blocks, they came with a wealth of suggestions, and these, too, we ignored. We assembled a number of simple vehicles because we could make wheels that actually rotated. Mr. and Mrs. Tinkertoy would not have approved, but at one point I assembled a machine gun and pointed it at Kath. My father witnessed my assault, and he didn't approve, either. He said I was waving a sharp object too close to my sister's eyes, and he smacked me on the head. I should have feigned blindness and sued him.

There was a studio couch in front of the picture windows in our living room—a narrow mattress with a brown and white slipcover and a dull green pleated skirt. Kath and I put Tinkertoy connector pieces on the ends of a half dozen Tinkertoy sticks and then pushed the sticks between the mattress and the frame below it. These became the instrument panel in the cockpit of an airplane that we flew.

Today when I watch a six-year-old playing video games on her iPad, I wonder how Kath and I could have been so engrossed in the remarkably simple amusements of our own childhood. But we were.

PEAR POINT

PICTURE MY FATHER in a defining moment. It's six-ish on a Saturday morning and he's standing, hands on hips, studying the half-filled trunk of our '50 Ford sedan. He's packing. And repacking. Suitcases and boxes first, then the smaller items; tucking and wedging and shifting and pulling things back out. He is, after all, a mathematician, and there must be a most efficient nesting with the rightness of a proof, but when he finally presses down with his palms to close the trunk it's anyone's guess whether he'll be satisfied, or haunted by what might have been.

As his son, I would one day be drawn to equally unrewarded tasks, but I twitched with impatience as I watched him then, because I was anxious for us to be on our way to a place that was enchanting to both of us, to our whole family. A place that offered a small child a dazzling choice of adventures. And when I was four and five and six years old, this place was so much bigger than I was that all its treasures could never be discovered. Seven acres of waterfront property on San Juan Island in Puget Sound. Seven acres of rock domes made pillow-soft by moss and lichen and tangled blackberry canes in subdued light under pine trees. And a thousand feet of shoreline with miniature rock peninsulas, small coves, gravel beaches and storm-hurled

5

logs. One of the peninsulas was labeled Pear Point on navigational charts, so that's what my father called our seven acres. He bought the land for $2,500 in 1953, and we spent all our summer vacations there until we moved to California in 1958, and returned a few times after that. Every feature of the land and water became imprinted on my soul, and I won't be surprised if I see them again as I draw my last breaths.

We'd all gotten up way too early so we could drive from Seattle to Anacortes to catch the first of the morning ferries to the San Juans. The sun through the living room windows was rich with yellow as Kath and I groggily spooned our cereal. Our mother and our older sister, Judy, bustled in the kitchen while my father attended to his pre-departure rituals outside. Finished with the trunk, he'd be working on the trailer, covering it with an army surplus tarp, criss crossing the tarp with rope cinched so tight a hurricane couldn't tear it loose. Then, finally, he was done and we could leave.

There were few other cars on the road as we drove north on Highway 99, as if we alone were privy to a wonderful secret. I was quietly buzzing with anticipation, peering out the back windows as the morning brightened. I would never feel more cozy and secure.

After two hours we turned west at Mt. Vernon,

leaving the main highway for the two-lane road that ran through farm country to end at the ferry terminal in Anacortes. My father parked our car in the boarding lane for Friday Harbor and walked to the terminal building to buy a ticket. Then we waited for twenty minutes or an hour, the car buffeted by onshore gusts and seagulls squawking overhead until uniformed men blew whistles and windmilled their arms to advance the lanes in the proper order. The front and rear wheels on each car *cu-clunked* as they dropped from the terminal ramp to the car deck on the ferry. We *cu-clunked* three times, twice for the car and once for the trailer, then crept into the echoing hollow of the car deck, stopping inches from the rear bumper of the car in front of us.

Island residents often napped in their cars until they disembarked, but to us the ferry ride was nearly as special as our destination, so we climbed one of the metal stairways to the enclosed passenger deck. There were long rows of banquettes next to the windows, and we laid claim to one of them, although I wasn't yet ready to sit. I would stand at the stern as the ferry churned away from the landing, watching the pilings and white fuel tanks in Anacortes grow smaller as we crossed the open water of Rosario Strait.

Later, I might stand outside at the bow, my face

square to the cold wind like a Viking on the North Atlantic. I'd watch for a dot moving toward us on the water, a white-and-green object slowly taking the form of another ferry headed our way. As the two boats passed close by, the passengers on each one looked at the passengers on the other. For a split second, we were precisely aligned.

When I rejoined my family inside, there would be snacks on the table and maybe a deck of cards, but to me the scenery was always more compelling. We passed south of steep Cypress and Blakely Islands, then close by low Decatur with its sandy beaches, anchored sailboats and occasional houses peeking out through the trees. The water was often flat in these narrow passages, where seabirds drifted with the tide and sunlight glinted on wet strands of kelp. The ferry rumbled with the vibration of its powerful engines. The windows shuddered quietly in their casements. We drowsed.

The first stop was Upright Head on Lopez Island, and I went outside to watch. I'd heard that ferry pilots occasionally misjudged their approach and took out a set of pilings, and I was keen to see how this was done, but we were moving slowly—the wind and currents apparently taken into account—and just when things looked promising, the pilot reversed the front screws to nudge the dock like a kiss on the cheek.

Crewmen trotted out to loop enormous hawsers around enormous cleats, there was more whistling and windmilling, and a stream of vehicles emerged below me to *cu-clunk cu-clunk* off the ferry and up the ramp. A milk truck and a tow truck and a van full of Wonder bread drove off the boat as if they were on a city street.

The ferry stopped next at Orcas Island, then headed for Shaw Island. En route to Shaw, it turned 180 degrees so that when it arrived, the cars disembarking wouldn't have to back off the boat. Friday Harbor on San Juan Island was the final stop. In anticipation, we gathered up our things and trooped back downstairs to sit in the car until the ferry docked. I found it odd to be moving in a car that was standing still, at least in relation to the cars around it, but this was just one of several oddities that I (and probably no one else) saw in the relationships between mainland and water and island. The checker in Saunder's Market, for example, rang up our groceries just like a checker in Seattle. Was it possible he hadn't noticed that he lived surrounded by Puget Sound?

It was three miles on a county road from Friday Harbor to Pear Point, to the overgrown gate at the head of an overgrown driveway few people would have noticed. My father drove in slowly and carefully, dodging the worst of the bumps and holes, and inching between tree trunks for a hundred yards until we stopped thirty feet short of the water. We were back.

Back, in the first years, to the land, the shore, the water and just two improvements—a loosely constructed fire pit above the high-tide line and a toilet seat on a five-gallon bucket. We kept our fresh water in a huge army surplus soup tureen that my father periodically filled at the Union 76 station in town. We wriggled into army surplus sleeping bags in an army surplus tent that was thick with the aroma of treated canvas, and uninhabitable in direct sun. We wetted our toothbrushes in salt water and bathed quickly in the bone-aching cold of the Sound. The outside world was no longer a boundless arena into which we ventured for an hour or an afternoon if it wasn't too cold or dark or wet. Instead, we lived all day under the sky, and gathered around the fire on wind-chilled evenings. We sat on logs. We listened as the waves tongued the rocks.

To me, Pear Point was a place of margins—between water and beach, beach and meadow and then meadow and forest, and finally between what was ours and what was not: our fenced property along the west side of the county road and Art Crosby's fenced pastureland to the east. I would come to know all of these, but in the beginning I spent my days near the water with my parents and my sisters. My mother would often be there—cooking, heating dishwater over the fire, combing the beaches, relaxing in the sun—and she kept Kath and me within sight. I was a timid child frightened by doctors, dogs, escalators and thunder, but my fears were no match for the pleasure of scrambling over rock outcroppings perfectly textured to hold the soles of my sneakers without scraping my hands. The logs that became bridges connecting some of these outcroppings were like fat tightropes. I didn't tense as I crossed them, although my last few steps were quick ones. My parents, who typically reacted to my timidity by being overprotective, sensed my confidence and granted me unaccustomed freedom.

Our front yard in Seattle ended at the shore of Lake Washington, so I knew life next to water, but Pear Point was different. The vista was grander. It was three or four miles across the water to Lopez Island and fifty to the crisp white face of Mt. Baker. To our right, the southern third of San Juan Island curved around to end at Cattle Point, likewise several miles away. We could often see the glaciers on the Olympic Mountains floating in the haze. I savored this spaciousness when I was old enough to notice it, and if I felt more exposed than protected, I could always drop down into one of the little beaches.

The advance and retreat of the tides was new to me. As the incoming flow eased up the beach, the configuration of the waterline around the rocky peninsulas changed from moment to moment. Knobs of rock became stepping-stones that grew smaller as I watched. Hollows became tiny lakes. Channels filled until they were too wide to jump.

I thought the creatures that lived underwater were meant to remain underwater, and high tide was, therefore, the natural order of things. Exploring during a low minus tide made me vaguely uneasy because when the water returned it would certainly be over my head, and what was to prevent it from rushing back all at once? Where, for that matter, had it all gone? Despite these worries, I toured the usually inaccessible terrain. We all did, even my father, who rarely allowed himself to spend vacation time unproductively. Our family could be seen early on a gray morning, moving slowly and carefully among tide pools. We carried a bucket to serve as a momentary aquarium for the most intriguing animals, which, for my money, didn't look like animals at all. None of them had fur or feet or tails, and some of them didn't even move. But how wonderfully strange they were! Huge starfish with too many legs to count. Sea anemones that were flowerlike in their squishy way, and spiked sea urchins like medieval weapons. And sea cucumbers and tube worms and the weird gum-shoe chiton, a cross between half a cantaloupe and a catcher's mitt.

As the tide rose my focus shifted to the beaches, which were mostly gravel—small multicolored stones worn to the shapes of olives and jelly beans and flattened eggs. Kath and I gathered the prettiest of them when they were wet and glossy, then tossed them back after they dried. We dug pits in the gravel and populated them with little grey-green crabs that scuttled unfailingly back to the water. We roamed from one little beach to the next, sometimes together, more often alone, collecting all sorts of things that had washed ashore, many from the decks of fishing boats. We found net floats that looked like cork donuts or small wooden footballs. And a few Japanese blown-glass floats that my mother kept because she liked their watery colors. I found two ration kits, which I assumed were artifacts from the Second World War until my father pointed out that there were often troop maneuvers on a nearby island.

Some stretches of beach beyond all but the highest tides were covered with driftwood, from finger-sized sticks and wayward planks to massive logs that didn't move from one year to the next. All these former trees and scraps of lumber had been rounded to friendly shapes and bleached by the sun. They were versatile. I could bang one piece of driftwood against another to make noise, or use it like a baseball bat to whack stones out into the Sound. Conversely, I could toss a piece into the water, imagine it to be a German battleship and bombard it with stones. At night, after the cooking fire had settled to a bed of coals, I would load some of them onto a little driftwood barge, launch it carefully out onto the water and pelt it until it capsized and the coals sizzled and winked out. There's a lot to be said for a beach if you like to throw things.

My parents found uses for the driftwood, too, though they were more practical than entertaining—log rounds rolled into place as seats, a wide board propped up near the fire pit to serve as a kitchen counter. The winter storms piled driftwood so generously around our cooking area that firewood was always within reach. I was never up early enough to build a fire before breakfast, but I coveted this chore before dinner— selecting an armload of wood and stacking it in criss crossed layers over balled newspaper, pencil sticks first, chair legs last—so that a single struck match created a fierce bouquet of flames.

My mother cooked everything over an open fire, and it was challenging. Frying eggs could scorch quickly, and the slices of bread she set out to toast on hot rock slabs often charred while she focused on the eggs. But you could scrape the black stuff off the toast and slather on enough blackberry jam that it didn't matter.

The salts that driftwood absorbed as it floated in the ocean gave such intense flavor to meat that we barbequed almost every night. A juicy chuck steak was the best, I thought, and my mother agreed, but chicken and fresh salmon were also delicious. So was barbequed rabbit, when our neighbor, Ray Stephan, shot an extra one.

Ray was one of three men I'd heard my father speak of as a friend. He'd bought the land to the north of us and built a one-room cabin and then a house. He invited us to his barbeques and we invited him to ours, and sometimes he arrived carrying a bottle of wine and sometimes he brought a limp rabbit. My mother would open the wine or take the rabbit out to the edge of the water, cut off the head, skin it, gut it and toss the entrails into the Sound. There were a great many rabbits on San Juan Island in the '50s. An early resident, it was said, either lost or set loose some Belgian hares, and the hares interbred enthusiastically with their native cousins. At dusk, you could see dozens of rabbits hopping on Art Crosby's land, or sitting on the county road absorbing the last of the day's warmth. No license was required to hunt them, nor much skill. You sat by the side of the road with a .22 rifle until one of them wandered within range, whistled so that it rose to attention on its hind legs, fired a round and collected your dinner.

Ray took me hunting once or twice, and then my father did, too, perhaps because Ray had an awful temper and my father had second thoughts about me spending time with him when he was armed. Once, he borrowed Ray's rifle, and the two of us sat comfortably in shaded woods in the middle of the day, a place and time remarkably unsuited to hunting rabbits, even on an island infested with them. My father soon fell asleep, and while he snored quietly, a handsome four-point buck pranced through the trees less than fifty feet away. I told my father when he woke up, but he didn't believe me. We hunted properly a second time, sitting on the verge of the road just before sunset. My father said—several times—that the rabbits were too far away, but he fired a few rounds over their heads for effect before we headed back to camp.

I understood my father's reluctance to kill an animal, and I respected it. I often felt that way, too. What I didn't understand was why he didn't choose to spend more time with me—or with any of us—in other ways. He spent nearly all his days at Pear Point working on a succession of projects. The first one had been to improve the road to the water. He cut and pruned trees, hauled gravel and leveled axle-busting rocks with a sledgehammer so we wouldn't have to lug everything over the footpath from Ray's driveway to our campsite.

He built a tent frame with half-height walls so we could stand up inside, and the next summer he converted it into a cabin with bunk beds and a window. All these were welcome comforts, and I think he enjoyed the work even as he felt compelled to do it, but there were nights he hammered by the light of a Coleman lantern while the rest of roasted marshmallows. What was the hurry?

I slept in the cabin when it rained, but the bunks were hard and narrow. I preferred a hammock strung between two pine trees just outside. I was out in the open, getting a feel for independence. I could hear the ancient music of water lapping against rock. Fishing boats passed by at first light, headed for open water. I heard the pucka-pucka-pucka of their engines and the voices of the men on board, unintelligible across the water. If I opened one eye, I could see the sunrise.

When I was older and free to explore at will, I wandered among the pocket meadows back from the water. They were bounded by trees and thickets and domes of rock lavishly upholstered with pale green lichen. Judy would retreat to these meadows to read or sunbathe away from the wind and the glare off the water, but even though I was drawn to their stillness and solitude, I was restless, moving from one to the next as if they were galleries in a museum.

I turned nine at Pear Point in August, 1958. Later that month we followed a moving van from Seattle to Northern California. My father had tired of the growing urban congestion and worried that Seattle—home to Boeing—would be a fat target in a nuclear war. I understood these concerns, but I didn't want to leave our big front lawn with the house at one end and the lake at the other and flower-brightened rockeries along each side. Had I considered what it would mean to live a two-day drive away from Pear Point, I would have chained myself to the front door of the house.

After the move, I began to dream that my father was packing the car and the trailer—packing and unpacking and repacking until I woke up with a lump in my throat. And then, a few summers later, we were on our way north with so much gear in the trailer that the Ford's engine overheated on the long uphill grade south of the Collier Tunnel and we got a push from a highway patrolman. And it was the same. We *cu-clunked* on and off the ferry—a bigger, faster one—and worked our way down the familiar jungled driveway to that first, heart-swelling glimpse of blue Sound sparkling through the trees. The views were the same, Mt. Baker was the same, and the shapes of the rock outcroppings were just as we had left them.

What had changed, though at first I didn't notice, was that I was seeing it all now as a boy close to adolescence. The shoreline that had once invited a whole morning's exploration was now a five-minute walk. The vetch near the fire pit no longer charmed me with its purple flowers. The wind and the bright light were fatiguing. And there were other changes independent of my waning childhood. The water, once startlingly clear, was now blurred by silt from the gravel pit near town. There were plastic bottles on the beaches and trash left by trespassers who had camped on our land in our absence. Kath and I were moody and remote. We occasionally sat together raking our fingers through the gravel looking for beach glass, but more often she lay in the sun next to her transistor radio. I found it strange and depressing to hear "Light My Fire" on the same beach where we'd once had a crustacean petting zoo, but Kath was living in the present. I longed for the simple pleasures of our past.

Fifteen years after my father bought Pear Point, it was worth much more than $2,500. He was paying that much in property taxes every three or four years, and now he had one kid in college with another soon to follow. He began to talk about selling the land or donating it to the Nature Conservancy. I think in part he was needling us, reminding us who signed the checks for what we thought of as ours. But we no longer traveled to Pear Point, and then, suddenly, my father had a fatal heart attack, and Pear Point was not just a remembered childhood world, but the most wrenching evidence that all my worlds had been essentially fatherless. I began to have another dream: I was suspended over the Sound by dream-world physics, looking down on our land, which was dotted with other people's houses. A road ran along the shore, and there were strangers on the beaches.

A year or two after my father's death, my mother and I drove to Seattle to visit old friends, and we spent a day at Pear Point while we were in the area. Later, I went there by myself. I took a bus from Seattle to Anacortes, rode the ferry to Friday Harbor and walked with my backpack from town to Pear Point. I found beer bottles outside the cabin, and someone had jimmied the lock. The air was so hazy I couldn't see across to Lopez, and while I sat numb on the cabin steps, two teenagers motored past in an open boat, firing a rifle into the trees. One of the bullets thrummed within earshot. I wept, head in hands, and thought that if I walked quickly back to town I could catch the next ferry to Anacortes and not have to spend the night.

My mother eventually sold Pear Point to a retired couple from Los Angeles for $250,000, a hundred times what my father paid to buy it. With the money, she was able to send us postcards from several continents, and, because she was generous, she helped Judy and her husband buy a house, helped Kath go back to school, and helped me buy a car and spend a month in Nepal. For their part, the new owners built a house back in the trees. They paved the driveway and planted flowers. They fixed up the cabin as a playhouse for their grandchildren. It seemed right to me that they would see every day what we had seen at most two weeks a year. They said we were always welcome to visit the land.

Sometimes I daydream about what I would do if I won the lottery. I used to think I would buy Pear Point back, or find a similar stretch of waterfront where I could keep the shore and the Sound a part of my life. But in a way they already are. Every step I've taken on the bare rock of the High Sierra or Greenland or Arctic Canada is in part a return to my clambering on the rock at Pear Point.

I went back one last time with friends from Seattle. We had warm weather, clear skies and clear water, and we barbequed chuck steak over driftwood coals. It was a wonderful visit, but when it was time to leave, I thought about my father. I was close to tears most of the way back to Anacortes.

A Brief Tide Pool Guide

Barnacles are loyal friends
Who seldom drift away.
Oysters, though, can be aloof
And hold their friends at bay.

Anemones are hard to please
And flounders love to flirt.
Clams have short attention spans
And octopuses squirt.

Kelp can help around the house
(The simpler chores are best).
The tide pool pranks of nudibranchs
Put patience to the test.

The Great Northwestern Geoduck
Has only got one foot. It
always wears its shoe because
There's no place else to put it.

The many legged starfish
Is both thoughtful and polite.
She'd never phone an abalone
After nine at night.

OVER THE RIVER AND THROUGH THE WOODS

MY UNCLE ALVIN, AUNT ELOISE AND THREE COUSINS lived for many years in a small community east of San Francisco. We rarely saw them while we lived in Seattle, but after we moved to Arcata, we regularly drove down for a visit, my father at the wheel, my mother riding shotgun, and Kath and I in the back. (Judy was in college up in Seattle.) Even then, there were seat belts all around, for in prudence if nothing else my father ran at the head of the pack.

We began by traveling south on Highway 101 through what was then known as the Redwood Empire. In all, it was an nine-hour drive—a long time for two kids to entertain themselves, let alone refrain from passing wind as our father expected us to do. Kath and I sometimes kept watch for license plates from New Mexico or Tennessee, but I was more inclined to gaze out the windows as we drove past familiar landmarks. The highway south of Eureka threaded for fifty miles through groves of old growth redwoods along the South Fork of the Eel River. These trees were so tall and massive, so much bigger than anything I encountered in my daily life, that I had no standard by which to gauge their majesty as we passed beneath them.

Most of the hamlets that periodically interrupted 101's drowsy backdrop of river and forest comprised little more than a post office, a motel, a café, a bar, and often a tepee burner just outside of town—a huge, rusty, inverted thimble in which the local mill burned sawdust and scrap. On the highway, logging trucks grumbled north and south, bits of shed bark dancing on the pavement in their wakes. The oncoming trucks were a compelling sight as they snaked toward us through intervening curves with dark exhaust streaming from their stacks. They seemed sure to pile into us at lethal speed, and yet they always roared safely past. Years later, when I was working summers as a seasonal ranger at Richardson Grove State Park, I lived in a tiny cabin thirty or forty feet from 101. I fell asleep to the machine gun purr of southbound Kenworths and Peterbilts as their drivers activated their compression brakes for the downgrade outside my window.

We made our pilgrimages to the Bay Area during the age of roadside attractions, when those not content simply to admire the redwoods *au naturel* could pay to see The World's Biggest or Oldest or Tallest, and pay again to see for themselves that what God can create, man can improve: The Tree House, The Stump House, The Drive Thru Tree, all of them World Famous.

We never stopped to take in these wonders—our trip would be long enough as it was—but on our way back north I could at least look forward to The World's Most Persistent Billboards. Each one was proof that we were measurably closer to home, and I liked the combination of *Don't Miss It* graphics and rustic iconography. Among my favorites were the billboards for Trees of Mystery, a Class A tourist trap near the Oregon border where huge statues of Paul Bunyan and Babe the Blue Ox kept watch over the parking lot. These billboards had been placed at thirty- to forty-mile intervals along northbound 101 from the Bay Area to Humboldt County and beyond: an Indian brave tragically slumped on horseback, silhouetted against a Zane Grey sunset. THE END OF THE TRAIL, the billboards read. ONLY 170 MILES, ONLY 133 MILES, ONLY 85 MILES. I was pretty sure that California's Indian tribes didn't ride horses, and Paul Bunyan was born in Maine, but I was content to appreciate the overall effect.

Once, and only once, we visited the World Famous Shipwreck, which had conveniently run aground south of Eureka. It was little more than a galleon-shaped souvenir shop, and after we'd had a brief look inside and were returning to our car, we saw that one of the castaways was wiring a cardboard WE VISITED THE WORLD FAMOUS SHIPWRECK placard to the bumper of every car in the parking lot. My father immediately removed ours, but many people kept miniature billboards like these as vacation merit badges. WE VISITED THE PREHISTORIC GARDENS. WE VISITED UNDERSEA WORLD.

We usually stopped for lunch in Willits or Ukiah, two towns more or less halfway between Arcata and Uncle Al and his family. This was a high point for me because we ate in cafés only when we were traveling— my parents didn't share my fascination with their ambience. I understood their lack of enchantment with bad coffee and wilted lettuce, with the racks of knee-slapping postcards featuring Zeke from the Ozarks and his crescent moon outhouse, but I thought it was all great—the swollen burgundy banquettes, the yellow mustard dispensers that farted when you squeezed them, the grizzled locals who kept their counter stools warm while they spoke without urgency in two-pack-a-day rumbles. And especially the waitresses with their nylons swishing between plump thighs. I admired their purposeful bustling as they brought menus and glasses of water, balanced a table load of dishes on one arm, and remembered who ordered the open-faced turkey sandwich.

I was overwhelmed by the thought that I could order anything I wanted. I studied the menu as if it were one of those ads in *Boy's Life* that showed all the prizes you could win by selling just twelve boxes of lovely All Occasion greeting cards. The Daisy Air Rifle or the Super Cub Plane? The grilled ham sandwich or the French dip? I agonized for five minutes and then ordered what I always ordered, a cheeseburger medium rare.

Before we could sit down to eat, it was necessary for my parents to play a round of Pick the Restaurant. Here's how it worked. My father's role was to drive slowly down the main street. My mother's role as we approached each restaurant was to make a quick evaluation and say "Stop" or "Keep Going." The catch was that if she said, "Stop" and the service was slow or the meat was grey, she would be implicitly responsible. She knew that, just as she knew there might not be any options that met our family standards. So she waffled. We'd all see The Woodsmen's Lounge coming up on the right and she'd say, "Gee, it looks kind of expensive," and then it would be Low's Family Style Chinese, and she'd say, "Didn't we just have Chinese last week?" And then the Red Robin Café, which was—inconveniently—on the other side of the street. "Oh, I don't know, Orval. What do you think?"

This was my father's cue. "Jesus Christ, Rae," he would hiss. "Would you make up your mind?" But by then we'd be on the outskirts, with nothing but gas stations and boarded-up fruit stands on either side of the road, and he'd have to make a U-turn and try again. It was ungallant of me, but I shared my father's frustration with my mother's indecisiveness, and found the routine amusing until he boiled over. Once, after we'd passed three or four restaurants and the tension was spilling onto the back seat, I timed our approach to the next one and piped up, "Stop here!" Which, to my amazement, he did. I imagine he was grateful for a way out of such undignified silliness.

My parents are long gone now, and it is I who live in the Bay Area. Two or three times a year, I drive north to spend a few days with friends in the erstwhile Redwood Empire, now the North Coast. The mostly two-lane highway which once skirted hills and ridges is now a mostly four-lane freeway more inclined to confront them head on, so it's now a four-and-a half-hour drive with one pee stop. The cafés and the motels and the tepee burners are mostly gone. I don't especially miss them, or the older, slower road, although the engineering for the new one seems based, along some precipitous stretches, more on faith than physics, and the annual Storm of the Century often sends several thousand cubic yards of adolescent geology sluicing down a mountainside to close it for a month.

I've been up and down Highway 101 so often now that the sequences of straight stretches and curves and upgrades and downgrades, while not rote, are so familiar that I don't drive them so much as float along in a trance of remembrance. I know the vineyards of Sonoma County, the broad valleys of southern Mendocino, and the Eel River Canyon. I see them vary with the seasons and the weather, the floods and the droughts, but their essence will not change in my lifetime. They offer me a scaled-down version of the High Sierra, the bared ribs of the planet which assure me that my small triumphs and my worst failures will not long trouble the Greater Order.

Some Names Are Too Short

There once was a hungry giraffable
Whose neck was so short it was laughable
It grieves her a bunch
That she can't reach her lunch
But pie for dessert keeps her affable.

Her grocer, a spry kangarooter
Was approached by a naval recruiter
He was hard to resist
But she didn't enlist
Because frankly the pay didn't suit her.

Her broker, that lazy vamoose
Oversleeps at the slightest excuse
My alarm doesn't work
It's a troublesome quirk
The kadingaling spring must be loose.

Her dentist, an unabashed bocelot
Often badgers her patients to floss a lot

And to brush after meals
(What romantic ideals)
And to dine on spaghetti with sauce a lot.

Her lawyer, that silly gorillable
Asked his mom, can I bill by the syllable?
I would think, she replied
That you first must decide
Whether sneezes and coughs can be billable.

INSECTS

BUG. A CONCISE WORD. A blue collar word, not an NPR word. Most of us say bug when we mean insect, and sometimes the two are synonymous. A stink bug, for example, really is a bug, with a unique criss crossed way of folding its wings, and dozens of other buggish traits familiar to anyone to whom such distinctions matter. Ladybugs, however, are not bugs, but beetles, and at most half of them are ladies. The truth is, most insects are not bugs, they're wasps or dragonflies or crickets, but there are few rewards for such knowledge, and those who insist on sharing it risk eating their lunch alone in the sixth grade just like Henry Kissinger or Margaret Mead.

I had lunchmates in the sixth grade because I kept this sort of thing to myself. I was—discreetly—a Bayside Grasshopper, a 4-H member who collected insects. I'd been a Cub Scout for a year in Seattle and Kath had been a Brownie, but after we moved to California, our parents enrolled us in the Bayside Chapter of the 4-H Club, which met at the Grange Hall near our elementary school. I chose to study insects because we had no pasturage to raise a calf or a lamb, and because 4-H Entomology sounded more interesting than 4-H Electricity, which was my only other option.

Had I been a proper rookie entomologist, I would have learned about the many ways insects affect human enterprise—all that pollinating and chewing and stinging. I would have learned which insects should be counted as friends, and which should be squashed without mercy. And I did master the basics. I knew that to be a card-carrying member of the spectacularly unexclusive class Insecta, it was necessary to have six legs attached to a thorax, with a head at the front end and an abdomen at the back. That wings were common but not mandatory. That mouth parts could chew like a grasshopper's or suck like a mosquito's. Getting up to speed on these attributes allowed me to identify a silverfish or recognize the difference between a scorpionfly and a caddisfly, but I had no interest in any of these. They were drab and uncharismatic, like most of the pests that break the hearts of farmers and foresters with their ruinous eating habits.

My criteria for an insect worthy of attention were aesthetic, not economic, and the most important one was usually size. The bigger and more robust the insect, the more legitimate its claim to being a bona fide animal like a frog or a mouse instead of a trivial life form like an ant. (Though technically insects, ants are so small and commonplace I never thought to collect one. How would I have pinned it?) The pine sawyer, a handsome nut-brown beetle the size of an Almond Joy, was more my kind of insect. It had presence, and it was strong enough that if I held it between my thumb and forefinger I could feel its strength as it flailed its legs in an effort to escape. Small insects like flies can move at the speed of subatomic particles, but big ones often lumber along at an observable pace.

Jerusalem crickets—improperly called potato bugs, as I would have pointed out—were another favorite. A big one was the size of my preadolescent thumb and much pudgier than the elegant, leggy crickets that the Chinese keep in bamboo cages. Its colors ranged from a rich brown on top to a creamy beige underneath, and what made it so weirdly intriguing was that it had a damp, shiny translucence as if it had just molted and its new exoseleton hadn't yet hardened. Any girl worthy of the name would have screamed if she saw a Jerusalem cricket, but to me they had a kind of teddy bear huggability. Once, one of them squeezed under the French doors into our living room, and my mother, fond of all creatures great and small, put it in a glass jar with a small chunk of raw potato and a tiny container of water. Regrettably, potato bugs don't eat potatoes, and it died even before she'd named it.

Fuzziness was the second best characteristic after size. Consider the differences between a honeybee and a bumblebee. I admired honeybees—it's against the law not to—and I felt badly if I inadvertently stepped on one on the lawn, particularly if I was barefoot, but a honeybee simply doesn't have a bumblebee's commanding presence. It's too small and thinly clad. Bumblebees, on the other hand, wear striped black and yellow angora sweaters. I wanted to stroke them with my finger, but they were always too busy hovering and zooming.

Collecting insects is in some ways like collecting stamps or matchbooks. The collection is small at first; it grows; it gets organized and categorized; and certain characteristics are favored over others. But, unlike an airmail stamp from Peru or a matchbook from the Hotel George V, insects resist being collected—sometimes quite effectively—by flying away or scurrying to the nearest place of refuge. Or by biting or stinging or issuing nasty fluids. Stalking one, chasing it down and capturing it, embodied the hunting urge in miniature.

The Bayside Grasshoppers used butterfly nets to capture anything that flew, and more durable beating nets for sweeping through tall grass or whacking things loose from overhead branches. Each of us had a killing jar. The killing jar shown in my spiral-bound copy of *How to Know the Insects* was a corked bottle labeled CAUTION: POISON, with half an inch of cyanide-infused plaster of paris at the bottom. According to the text, "some compound of cyanide makes the best killing agent." According to our 4-H leader, eleven-year-old boys do not run around carrying cyanide in breakable containers. Instead, we each cut a round disk from one of our mother's kitchen sponges, stuffed it into an empty Skippy Peanut Butter jar and soaked it with carbon tetrachloride, which was less effective than cyanide but not life threatening to collectors.

Insects were everywhere, and we looked everywhere to find them—in backyards and open fields, around thickets of blackberry vines, and under boards and rocks. We tore apart rotten logs to see who might be living inside them, poked through manure piles and upended the carcasses of birds and gophers. Once, we came upon a dead cow with hordes of maggots roiling in its abdominal cavity and spilling out of its nostrils. That night, I dreamed that I was sweeping the desiccated shells of enormous beetles across the bare floor of an empty room.

The leader of the Bayside Grasshoppers was a sincere but edgy woman named Barbara, who wore blue jeans with four-inch cuffs, rimless spectacles, and carelessly applied red lipstick. She'd studied entomology in college and now lived in an unfinished house with her husband, Evan, a wonderfully kind man who anyone could see was an alcoholic though in fact he didn't drink. Evan worked as a mechanic at the Arcata Airport, but he lived to fish—surf fishing after work, steelhead on the weekends. Barbara kept him company on his fishing excursions along the Trinity River, and interested Grasshoppers were often invited to tag along as an informal field trip. I enjoyed these fine outings, leaving early on a Saturday morning with sandwiches and a big jug of Kool-Aid, heading inland on Highway 299 in a road-weary station wagon. They were some of my first adventures away from my family, and Evan was as relaxed and casual as my father was wary and reserved. He wore a greasy billed cap and somehow always had a two-day stubble. He steered with one hand as he rolled a cigarette with the other, creasing a paper, using his teeth to open a small cloth bag of Bull Durham, spilling out some tobacco, rolling a lumpy, spit-gobbered approximation of a cigarette, lighting it, and then parking the sodden mess at the corner of his mouth to smolder and spark until he was ready for the next one. Evan spoke little and barely parted his lips when he did, but his good nature snuck out.

It was hot and dry along the Trinity River, not at all like the fog-tempered coast, and the insects there were as different as the climate. Toad bugs and tiger beetles, horse flies and ominous bald-faced hornets. I caught an iridescent woodboring beetle so gorgeously green that I must have hesitated before I dropped it into my killing jar, and yet it was because it was so dazzling that I had to add it to my collection. We came upon other items of interest in places like Hoopa and Hobo Gulch. A rattlesnake; a naked, middle-aged woman cooling herself in a river backwater, open-thighed and unabashed; a stack of racy magazines in a prospector's cabin where we spent the night.

When I returned home from a field trip, I would sit at the dining room table and shake the booty from my killing jar out onto a paper towel. My mother, who was generally indifferent to my interests, often sat with me as I looked over the day's catch, and I would identify each insect and tell her where I'd found it. She learned along with me how to display them correctly. They were to be pinned—mounted, properly speaking—with long, thin, black No. 2 insect pins from Ward's Supply House. Mounted just so: through the center of a butterfly's thorax, to the right of center for a grasshopper, and, for beetles, not through the thorax at all but through the right wing cover over the abdomen. All specimens were to be mounted square to the pin. *Too much emphasis cannot be placed on neatness of mounting. A carelessly mounted collection is an eyesore.*

Insect pins are longer than the pins you push into

the wall of a department store changing room. This is so there will be enough room to accommodate the three paper labels that will be impaled beneath each insect. The top label was a sort of conventioneer's badge: *Hello, I'm a Fungus Gnat.* The middle one was a Where Found, presumably, in this case, *On fungus.* The bottom label noted the date of collection, the county and the collector. Each label had a black dot in the middle. If you stuck the pin through the three dots, the labels lined up. They were very small labels, and it took some forethought to get, say, *Predacious Diving Beetle* to fit on one of them.

Each summer, I entered my growing insect collection in the Humboldt County Fair to be displayed and judged on a long row of folding tables surrounded by prize-winning tomatoes, floral arrangements from local gardens and plein air watercolors of old barns.

My display cases at first were cigar boxes I'd spray-painted black, their glass tops hinged with electrical tape. But in my fifth and last year, I entered four 18"x30" wooden cases, each filled with grouped orders and families of insects I had painstakingly aligned like recruits on a parade ground. Almost all my entries earned purple First Place ribbons, and when I retired my killing jar, I donated my collection to the Humboldt County Agricultural Extension Service, where, conceivably, it served some useful purpose.

To conduct the everyday business of catching, killing and pinning, I wore a T shirt, jeans and high top sneakers, but on formal occasions I upgraded to my 4-H uniform: a white dress shirt, white cotton slacks two inches too short, a thin green necktie, and a green felt hat festooned with commemorative pins and stripes. These formal occasions were most often the monthly Community Club meetings at the Grange Hall, but in the spring each of us prepared and presented a Demonstration, a sort of illustrated talk theoretically intended to inform the public about a relevant aspect of our year's work. For example, Colleen Fehely, a Home Ec 4-H'er, gave a Demonstration she called Slippery Washcloths, and it seemed to me that the point was not so much for her to show the audience how to transform old washcloths into a pair of slippers for Grandma as it was for her to learn to speak in public without stammering or peeing in her pants.

One of my Demonstrations, which I deftly titled Control the Foreign Hitchhiker, concerned Japanese beetles. They were notorious pests in the early '60s, although not in Humboldt County, so I had to write a few letters to get a specimen. The essence of my talk was that Japanese beetles were bad, that you ought to learn to recognize them, that modern agricultural science was developing effective countermeasures, and you should always wash your hands after handling them. I supplemented my talk with several white, easel-mounted poster boards that summarized key points in stenciled black letters, and I included a few color illustrations to sex things up. My remarks, which I'd padded to the requisite three or four minutes, were memorized from first word to last and delivered with the relaxed demeanor of a motorist pulled over for doing 35 in a 25-mile-an-hour zone. But I didn't pee in my pants.

Today, I'd guess I notice insects more often than most people, but I have no desire to do anything more than admire them. Occasionally, I'll rescue a wasp that's banging its head against the inside of a window—capture it with a drinking glass and a thin sheet of cardboard and release it outside—and when I do, I think of my act as symbolic atonement. But I flatten mosquitoes without remorse. I suspect God created them on a Friday.

Some Names Are Too Long

There once was a plump hippopot
Who thought himself thin, but was not
He ate only reeds
And riparian weeds
Plus the truckloads of cookies he bought.

His cousin, a cross-eyed rhinocer
Drinks peppermint tea from a saucer
She's an odd looking beast
As her north eye looks east
And her south eye looks backward across her.

His nephew, a round armadill
Took a fall near the top of a hill
He tucked in his toes
And his tail and his nose
And he rolled all the way to Brazil.

His nieces, two tap dancing buffals
Are in bed with a case of the snuffles

Their doctors suggest
They get plenty of rest
And eat raspberry sherbet with truffles.

His uncle, that crafty baboo
Sold lawnmower parts at the zoo
Though profits were small
He invested them all
And retired outside Bos, Massachu.

Behind the Wheel

If I'm cruising down Highway 101 at ten or fifteen miles over the posted speed limit and some entitled brickhead cuts me off, I may think about leopard seals in Antarctica. The leopard seal is a ruthless predator. It will burst from the water to snatch a penguin off the ice, then jerk it so violently that it rips its body clean out of its skin. No one would cut in front of a leopard seal.

I enjoy driving. I suspect that the pleasure I find in acceleration and cornering can be traced back to our simian ancestors as they swung from limb to limb in the treetops of an Eocene jungle. I've steered and shifted and braked for over fifty years and several hundred thousand miles and I think I've got the hang of it. But this was not always so.

I was fifteen and a half when I first sat behind the wheel of my father's bullet-nosed '50 Ford. It was time for me to learn how to drive, a time neither my father nor I had especially looked forward to. He, I suspect, because he was tired of my sullen resistance to his authority, and I because I assumed that pretty much any new experience would be uncomfortable, if not scary.

As directed, I began Lesson 1 by inching along our straight and narrow driveway. The Ford had a manual transmission—*three on the tree* as my more know-ledgeable classmates would have it—so in order to coax it into motion, I had to let out the clutch some unknown distance and simultaneously feed the carburetor some unknown amount of gas. In response, the car would buck and lurch and stall. And buck and lurch and stall again. I suspected things were going more smoothly for the *three on the tree* crowd, and I wondered, as I often did, why self-assurance and grace were so elusive.

Lesson 2 took place on a Saturday morning at a sleep-blurred hour when we could have the Safeway parking lot to ourselves. Once I could engage the clutch without stalling, I crept around endless circles and figure eights, worrying that if I somehow lost control, we'd roar across the parking lot and into the store, sending shelves of canned peaches and mayonnaise clattering down the aisles.

For Lesson 3, My father drove us out to the pasturelands west of Arcata. The country lanes there were as straight and flat as our driveway and almost as sparsely traveled. I took my place at the wheel and began driving down one of them at fifteen or twenty miles an hour, about as fast as we could go without racing the engine in first gear. OK, he said. Now shift into second. I took a deep breath, shifted as instructed, and—saints be praised—didn't drive us into a ditch.

I failed my first driver's test at the DMV. I didn't flatten any pedestrians, but the rumpled lifer who sat next to me with his clipboard said I was too hesitant. He might have been surprised if he'd seen me six months later, working on my elapsed time from the city limits to our house or nudging the speedometer up to 90 on the highway north of town. I drove fast, but each time only a little faster than the time before, and never faster than what I considered, based on thin experience, to be manageable. I made it through high school without running into anything more valuable than a garage door.

I liked the old Ford—the chrome starter button, the ivory knobs on the dashboard, the shape of the taillights and the clear Lucite fin on the hood. I remember that it had a friendly, broken-in smell, and I remember in particular that it was Sea Mist Green, because that was the color I painted it. With a brush. I'm pretty sure my father knew he could take his car to Earl Scheib and have it repainted for $39.99, but that knowledge didn't spare me the impossible task of concealing the car's original Royal Blue finish, never mind my brushstrokes, with the single quart of paint he'd bought at Western Auto.

My father dropped Kath and me off at Arcata High

each morning, stopping square in front of the second floor breezeway, the reviewing stand where lettermen and their toadies hung out before first period. I was sure they were sneering at my paint job, and at me.

I didn't own a car during my college years, and that was fine because I didn't need one and couldn't have afforded it in any case. I got my first vehicle when I was twenty-five—my father's '63 GMC pickup, which I bought from my mother for $700 after he died. It had a handmade camper shell, a Barden bumper and a V6 with pistons the size of coffee cans. It also had *four on the floor*, but little else in common with, say, a '65 Chevy Malibu except four wheels and a spare tire. I drove the truck for seven years and never washed or waxed it. I backed into a few things, scraped a few others and parked out of necessity in the sun so that the Fiberglas coating on the camper shell eventually began to slough off chunks the size of potato chips. Approaching drivers took note of the overall effect, ascribed it to some combination of bad depth perception and bad attitude, and proceeded with caution. This simplified left turns into traffic.

Aside from its potential for intimidation and its hearty exhaust note, there was little about the truck to warrant my affection. I drove it as long as I did only because it was easier than selling it and buying something else. When I'd finally had it with the window that wouldn't roll up all the way and the door that wouldn't shut all the way and the aerobic steering wheel, I began thinking about cars—cars I wanted to drive and cars I could afford to buy. They were all sports cars, like the red bathtub Porsche my favorite English teacher drove, a college classmate's vintage Jaguar XK140, and the Lotus Europa.

I procrastinated for months and then bought the first car I test drove, a vintage Porsche 912 with a brand new silver paint job. For about the same money, I could have had a considerably more powerful 911, but I was afraid I would wrap it around a tree. As it was, I quickly got two speeding tickets.

As much as I liked the Porsche's classic styling, I felt self-conscious driving it. In the pickup, I'd been essentially invisible. Now, I was afraid that other drivers would see me as materialistic, which I wasn't, or regard my car as a penis extender, which of course it was. But except for women in Volvo station wagons who passed me on principle, no one seemed to notice me at all. There were Porsches everywhere in Marin County, most of them much newer than mine. And teenaged boys advised me more than once that a 912 wasn't a real Porsche, just a streamlined Volkswagen with an extra carburetor.

The 912 was basic transportation. No power steering or power brakes or power windows. It had a heater that sucked heat off the engine if it was in the mood, and a useless defroster. These last features were annoying, but I liked the monastic simplicity. Friends who gave me grief for not owning a microwave oven or a dishwasher agreed that my Porsche and I were made for each other.

I washed and waxed the 912 at reasonable intervals, but, like the pickup, it spent its days out in the weather, and the silver paint gradually dulled and roughened. Rust began to appear around the headlights and the windshield. Water found its way in when it rained. I sponged out the car after the heaviest storms, but the floor mats stayed wet and stinky for months. Tiny mushrooms grew in protected corners. And there were ruinous assaults on my checking account for a new clutch, a transmission overhaul and major surgery on the front suspension.

When the car began to burn oil, I began to think about selling it. I wanted something more planet-friendly and cheaper to maintain. Several friends drove Hondas, and all of them talked about how dependable they were. I'd always associated Hondas with sensible shoes, but I thought I should consider a used Prelude, a practical car with modest aspirations to style. So I asked my friend, Ron, if I could drive his on our way to an A's game. It was faster than my 912 and it handled well, but every time I stepped on the gas, the engine went *phnnhhh*. No burbles or howls. No boy noises at all.

Soon after, as I wandered around European Auto Service waiting for the owner's diagnosis of my 912's latest ailment, I noticed a car mostly shrouded by canvas. I always checked out the other Porsches in the shop—the different colors, the subtle changes between model years, the flawless restorations. When the owner, Fred Jung, approached me, presumably with bad news, I asked him about the car under wraps. "Zat car belonks to Professor Steinmetz," he said. "He pot it in Chairmany in 1970, ent he has driven it effer since. Now he is vishing to sell it because his vife is olt ent cannot anymore get in ent out." He pulled back the canvas. It was a tomato red 911T with the crests of six European countries bolted to the bonnet. I'd promised myself I'd never drive a red Porsche. I thought the crests were a crime against design. I asked Fred how much he thought the car was worth. He said about $9,500. I called Professor Steinmetz. He said $11,000. I said I'd been thinking more along the lines of $9,000. We settled on $9,500.

The 911T was agreeably faster than the 912, and the rumble of the engine became a feral snarl at redline. And it was a five speed, so I could shift more often. I drove it for seven years and doubled the mileage before I got rear-ended in stopped traffic by a local poet driving a Suzuki Samurai. She maimed both of our cars and, while she was at it, the Mercedes sedan between us. My insurance company gave me six grand for the car, which, like the 912 before it, had become a mobile hothouse for diminutive fungi. I put a few thousand more miles on it and then bought a flawless, low mileage, red Mazda Miata that had never left its owner's garage except for trips to the Wine Country on warm weekends.

The Miata was another base price model. No leather, no air conditioner, no alloy rims. It had a radio, but I never used it because the instruction manual was in French and German. I drove it in silence for fourteen years and got 169,000 miles out of the original clutch. Then I bought red Miata #2, which, like red Miata #1, had low mileage. I drove it for several years and would have driven it many more but for a freak accident that left me dangling from my seat belt in an upside down car in two inches of muddy water. I wasn't hurt, but the car was totaled.

Enter Miata #3. It's black, with a retractable hardtop and a six—count 'em—speed transmission. And it's a Club Edition, which means it has more power and a stiffer suspension than Miatas #1 and #2. My niece said, "Unky, I don't see you in a black car," and I agreed, but it had been for sale at the Mazda dealership five miles from my house, and I hate to shop. I've since gotten used to the color.

Marin County is about 70 percent open space, most of it hilly terrain, so there are many secondary roads to wiggle around on. One of them snakes around the west flank of Mt. Tamalpais and then down to Alpine Lake and over to Fairfax. Now that I'm retired, I head up there once in awhile during the afternoon commute, when the Highway Patrol is busy ticketing sole occupants in the HOV lanes in Corte Madera. The speed limit is mostly 35, but there are tight turns I find interesting at half that speed as well as short stretches good for 50 or 55. I settle into a rhythm—left, right, left, right, brake, throttle, brake, throttle, hairpin. Sometimes I drive to the top of the mountain to take in the view—I can see the HOV lane in Corte Madera.

Before I retired, I took the bus to work unless I needed my car to drive to a meeting, which meant commuting in rush hour traffic. If I'd had a daily two or three hour commute, I would have been as harried as everyone else, but I thought of my occasional stints in stop-and-go congestion as opportunities for guilt-free indolence. When I was at work, I took my job seriously, assuming that the success of the firm depended on my unrelenting efficiency. Away from work, I felt compelled to make constructive use of my free time. I wrote, or brooded about not writing. I read *Newsweek* thinking I should finish Stephen Hawking's book instead. But, stuck in gridlock, I was a happy man.

During the winter, I had driven home in darkness as part of the opposed streams of headlights and taillights that undulated through the Marin hills. The darkness veiled the drivers around me and muted the differences between us. I was one of many corpuscles flowing through an artery, and I felt an odd sense of community.

Some Names Are Just About Right

The clockodile stares into space
As his hands move in front of his face
It's tempting to doze
As they spin on his nose
So he sets his alarm just in case.

When pantalope roam on the range
They frequently stop to exchange
Their hand-tailored trousers
With like-minded browsers
A custom their tailors find strange.

The scaribou sneaks up behind
With intentions completely unkind
But she's so indiscreet
With her big clumsy feet
That her victims don't usually mind.

Their friendship can undergo strain
When reigndeer debate who should reign

Now Bea, Blanch and Smitty
Could rule by committee
But everyone else would complain.

Despite what you might well suspect
The wrongoose is often correct
If you seek you will find
An astonishing mind
But it's fiendishly hard to detect.

TOY STORIES II:
THE WOLVERENE [SIC] CHEWS THROUGH LOGS
A FOOT THICK

It's the caption for the frontispiece of the children's book *Homes and Habits of Wild Animals,* published in 1934. The chewed-through logs are part of a cabin left vacant for the winter. Or maybe the owner is out checking his trap lines. The wolverine is crouching in the snow, tearing into a side of bacon.

I'd seen this illustration when I was very young because Judy had a copy of the book. Decades later, when I found a copy at a garage sale and saw the wolverine, it triggered a fleeting return to early consciousness that startled me. I don't remember anyone reading the book to me, and none of the other illustrations look familiar, but the wolverine, the logs and the bacon are a perfect match to an image that's been hibernating within me for sixty years.

I've kept a few other books from my preliterate childhood, books I pored over or flipped through or ignored depending on the character of their depicted worlds. One of them is *The Little Train.* The illustrations are grey charcoal drawings with occasional highlights of brown. The locomotive, the train station and the nearby farmhouses have the rounded shapes of toys, and the plump citizens of Tinytown seem busy but content. I envied them.

Kath and I had two large-format books that beckoned to us from a wider world: *The Golden Geography: A Child's Introduction to the World* and *The World We Live In*. I leafed through *The Golden Geography* many times. Each page had as many as a dozen vignettes. There were short paragraphs of text, too, but I saw them as mere compositional elements. The colors in the vignettes were advanced by Dick and Jane standards, each landmass a range of forest greens and chartreuses, each river a delicate greyed blue, the grasslands and deserts goldenrod and buff. I felt older just looking at them. One section, *Winds that Blow*, included an illustration with the caption "A Tornado" that fascinated me for years even though looking at it gave me the willies. There is a farmhouse on the right, its white porch a faint purple under the ominous sky. The blond father runs to the storm cellar on the left with his blond son in his arms. The mother and daughter are already inside; the mother reaches out to take the boy. The approaching tornado, a terrifying swirl of brown and yellow-green, looms on the horizon. A dog barks. Chickens scatter. A red wagon waits alone in the yard.

The World We Live In must have been intended for adults. It has whole pages of text. It has black-and-white photographs of adult subjects like galaxies and tidal marshes. But there are also many painstakingly detailed illustrations in color. The first of them shows a succession of earths curving toward me in darkness like a string of pearls. The ancient earth, red hot, emerges from a cloud of cosmic dust, rotating and cooling and growing larger until it is our earth—green, blue and white—with North America at the center. Then it curves away, heats up and disappears. This illustration got me thinking about eternity, which I dreaded because I assumed I would remain conscious after I died, floating forever in outer space with nothing to do. It also corrected a misconception I'd had about the nature of the earth's roundness. I thought the earth was a hollow sphere, that we lived *inside* on the bottom and the sky was the blue inner surface at the top.

The World We Live In has one other illustration that I had turned to many times—"The Great Age of Dinosaurs." Posed against cliffs and mountains and erupting volcanoes, a score of dinosaurs forage and lurch. Brontosaurus is present and accounted for. Tyrannosaurus Rex towers and glares as Triceratops munches at a safe distance. Allosaurus rips into a gory mass of flesh. Like any boy, I was enchanted by carnivorous mayhem, but this diorama also took me into the realm of geologic time.

When I had begun to read as well as look, my father gave me a copy of *Pogo's Peek-a-Book*, a sort of small-format comic book. He chuckled at the pointed whimsy Walt Kelly cooked up in Okefenokee Swamp, and though much of it sailed over my head, I thought it was pretty funny, too. One of my favorite pieces was "Suffern on the Steppes, or 1984 And All That," a satirical take on Soviet communism that featured Pogo as both ticket taker and locomotive for a derelict commuter train, and Owl as one of his apparatchik passengers. I knew nothing about communism or George Orwell, but it didn't matter. The drawings were clever and precise, the characters were endearing, and their dialogue and syntax were hilarious. In the first frames, Owl confronts Pogo at the ticket window. "Why is the 8:02 late? Why? I been waitin' a hour!" Pogo consults his schedule: "First of all, the 8:02 is been changed to the 10:39, so if it comes in at all today it'll be early." *How can you argue with that* I thought. Later, Owl searches his briefcase for the paper bag into which he'd hollered "Down with the gummint" in 1923. "Wanna see my holler?" he asks Pogo as he cautiously opens the bag. "Hooray for the gummint!" bursts out, startling them both. Owl regains his composure. "Naturally," he says, "I disguised it a l'il."

VEGETABLES

I DIDN'T LIKE THEM.

934 Fickle Hill Road

When my father met my mother on a blind date in the summer of 1946, he was living in a houseboat on Seattle's Lake Union. He had planned to move some of the interior walls around to make room for his army surplus jeep, fill up most of the rest of the space with books and records, buy a tugboat, tow the houseboat to southwestern Alaska, and bring culture to coastal communities inaccessible by road. No doubt many things seemed possible after the war had finally ended, and perhaps he thought that my mother, a full-blooded Finn, might be keen to hop aboard. She was not. But, on their third date, she happily accepted his proposal of marriage. Soon after, they bought a waterfront lot on Lake Washington, hauled the houseboat ashore, and lived in it while my father built a real house around it. It wasn't Alaska, but for the first winter, at least, he could knock icicles off the shower curtain each morning until he got the bathroom walled in.

I take all this on faith because I didn't show up until three years later, but I saw more than enough of another construction project after we moved to California. My father had accepted a teaching position in the mathematics department at what was then Humboldt State College in the town of Arcata. We rented a house near the campus and he began scouting around for a building site. He (or he and my mother, at least in theory) eventually bought ten acres three miles from town on Fickle Hill Road.

We would be able to see the Arcata bottomlands and Humboldt Bay and the ocean from our new home. There were a few houses nearby, but they were screened from us by trees—firs and alders, mostly, along with spruce and second growth redwoods. One of the redwoods was so tall we could see it from Highway 101. My father called it Lone Bill because he had a friend named Bill Lone. The truly massive old growth redwoods on our property had been logged decades earlier, leaving behind huge stumps eight or ten feet high that Kath and I—like kids all over the county—used as airy fortresses. Throw in a creek (my father called it Fickle Trickle), the meadows and a blackberry patch, and you had a sort of *Little House on the Prairie* without the midwestern winters.

But first we had to build that house, and I say *we* because that's what my father said. Actually, for the record, he didn't say. He asked: How would you like to help me build a house? What he meant, as my mother and Kath and I would soon discover, was how would you like to spend nearly every weekend and most of every summer doing the grunt work so we can live in the kind of house we could otherwise never afford on my salary as an associate professor? There was only one correct answer, and guess who was grading the papers.

The Fickle Hilton (yes, he came up with that one, too) was to be no ordinary house. My father believed that Western architecture had been defined too long by rectilinear geometry. He didn't propose to build a geodesic dome or a yurt, but the roof he had in mind would be one quarter of a hyperbolic parabola, a curved shape formed by straight lines. He enjoyed explaining that all the rain that fell on such a roof would drain at two opposite corners. What could be more distinctive than that?

It would be a big house—four thousand square feet on two levels including a two-car garage—and it would be substantial. There would be no conventional balloon framing with spindly 2x4s. Instead, it would be post and beam construction on a four foot by four foot grid, with 6x6 clear heart redwood posts, 6x6 diagonal bracing on either side of every picture window and double bracing at the corners. All the hallways sat square on the grid, so all the doors would be about three and a half feet wide. The front and back doors would be formed from 3x6 redwood tongue and groove bolted together with ½ inch diameter steel rods. If the next Big One sent our house tumbling down the hill, he'd just winch it back up.

My father adhered to one guiding principle while serving as his own contractor: Don't ask for anyone else's help if you can find a way, however time consuming and/or cumbersome, to keep the project in the family. Buying lumber, for example. The conventional way was to call the lumberyard and tell them you wanted fifty 16 foot 4x6s trucked to your building site. But if he did that, they'd pull the top fifty pieces off of a stack and charge to deliver them. So, first thing Saturday morning, he'd hitch up the trailer and he and I would drive to Copeland Lumber. We'd dismantle an entire stack of 4x6s to find the straightest pieces with the fewest knots, and then load them onto the trailer one by one. And unload them one by one when we got back. The salesmen at the lumberyard looked forward to our visits.

The 4x12 beams were much too big and heavy for this approach, so, reluctantly, my father had Copeland haul them up the hill and unload them at the top of our driveway, which was too steep and sinuous for a large truck. Then he brought in a work crew of fellow professors to help carry these beams down the hill. He insisted on writing each of them a check for fifteen dollars even though they likely considered the afternoon's work to be a sort of communal barn raising. Some of them refused to cash the checks, which meant that he couldn't balance the checkbook. It drove him nuts.

My father excavated for the perimeter foundation walls with a shovel and wheelbarrow, and erected plywood formwork one section at a time. The wet concrete was delivered and poured by a truck, and my mother and Kath and I tamped it endlessly to work out the air pockets and distribute the aggregate. In order to reuse the formwork, Kath and I scraped off the remnant dried concrete with putty knives. Then we hammered on the bent nails to straighten them out so that they, too, could be recycled.

When the concrete work was complete, my father began assembling wall sections on the floor slab and hoisting them into place with a block and tackle. The longer sections weighed hundreds of pounds, and raising one could take hours. It was a two-person job. My father operated a block and tackle, lifting the wall section inch by inch from horizontal to vertical like a huge hinge while my mother stacked and wedged pieces of construction scrap beneath it to hold the weight while he re-rigged. My father was cautious and systematic, and I'm sure he would have thought out all the steps in advance, but either he couldn't communicate them clearly to my mother or the taut rope made him nervous, because sooner or later he'd be barking at her. "Jesus Christ, Rae! Not that one, the other one."

It took more than five years of weekends and

summer vacations to complete the first floor so that we could move in while my father worked on the second floor. Kath was essentially off the hook after the concrete work was done, because my father couldn't come up with many suitable tasks for a nine-year-old girl. But there was always work for me to do, and I resented it. Looking back, I wonder if I might have been more willing to help if my father had made me his apprentice and taken pride in teaching me what he knew. What if he'd allowed me to drive nails and tighten bolts and chisel notches? These relatively glamorous tasks took no more strength than carrying one end of a beam or a bag of cement, things I did often. But instead I was given the Sisyphean task of maintaining our crude driveway, shoveling gooey clay out of the drainage ditches and raking the gravel back into the many potholes so the bouncing, skidding tires of my parents' cars could spit it back out again. I carried heavy loads of firewood up to the house from the creek bed below. I tarred the temporary roof every summer. I helped my mother prime and paint all the ceilings, using brushes instead of rollers so we could work the paint into the joints between the tongue and groove planks. Every ceiling was the same Sea Foam Green. The paint dripped on our faces and into our hair.

My father and I began fighting an undeclared war

of passive aggression. He'd asked, years before, if I wanted to help build the house, I'd naively nodded my head, and he expected the agreement to be honored, just as he did when Judy pledged—in junior high—that she would never smoke. When, pledge notwithstanding, she started smoking in college, he waved it in her face and wouldn't let it drop. He gave her lighters and ashtrays as Christmas presents for several years. Now he wanted my help, but he wouldn't ask for it. I didn't want to oblige because I thought he expected too much. I wanted to punish him for making me feel guilty if I read a book or listened to a Giants game while he was outside pounding nails. It became my mother's unhappy chore to coax and plead until I presented my father with my long face and reluctant hands. There were often days when the air in the house that he surely intended to be a gift to his family was thick with resentment, and no one spoke more than necessary.

When the house was finally complete there would be four bedrooms and two bathrooms upstairs, along with the kitchen, the dining room and a living room that spanned two time zones. In the meantime, the downstairs recreation room served as our living and dining rooms, the laundry room became a temporary kitchen, and my parents slept in what would someday be my mother's painting studio. Kath and I had temporary bedrooms in the garage—raw plywood walls and a bare concrete floor. I had a small window on an outside wall. Kath's window opened onto what remained of the garage. I didn't mind the austerity because, at fourteen, I finally had a room to myself. In Seattle, I'd slept in a crib behind a brocaded screen in my parents' bedroom, and then on a fold-up bed in the workshop off the kitchen. I did have a bedroom in each of the two rental houses where we lived before we moved into the Fickle Hilton, but I had to share it with the stacked cartons of kitchen cabinets and bathroom fixtures my father had bought at closeout sales.

I had a steel navy surplus bunk in my room, along with an old store counter, a night table and a broken refrigerator that I used to store my books. I carefully painted them all Chinese red and black. I bought rattan flooring at International Imports. I had a shortwave radio and tuned into English language broadcasts from cities like Lima and Johannesburg. I listened to the Top 40 on KRED—"The Night Has a Thousand Eyes," "Don't Say Nothin' Bad About My Baby," "Our Day Will Come," "Rhythm of the Rain." I assembled and customized scale model cars, drew imaginary floor plans, and copied photos of Haida masks. My bedroom was a showcase for self-expression and a refuge from the world.

We lived in the Fickle Hilton during my last three years of high school. I dashed to the heater outside the kitchen to dress for school on cold mornings. I split firewood for the Franklin stove and let the dog and the cats in and out. Kath and I lay on our parents' bed to watch *Get Smart* and *The Man from U.N.C.L.E.* and *Hogan's Heroes*. When I left for college in 1967, the house was unfinished, and it was still unfinished eight years later when I got an unexpected call from my mother. "Stanton," she said, "Dad's gone."

It was a Saturday morning, and he'd been pulling weeds in his potato patch in a small field above the house. He didn't want breakfast when he came back down. He had chest pain, and it was getting worse. He knew what it was, and my mother was pretty sure, too, but he refused to go to the hospital. Just let me die, he said. He might have been thinking about his friend, Ray, who had died many years before after unsuccessful heart surgery. Or about his mother, who wasted away in a nursing home. But the pain was terrible and at last he relented, and my mother helped him out to the car. She'd been a Pink Lady at Mad River Community Hospital for years. She knew the drill.

He had a heart attack in the emergency room, but they pressed paddles to his chest and his heart began beating again. He thought he'd been struck by lightning. He told my mother he'd been having chest pains for a year, and she knew then why he'd signed up for more life insurance. He told her not to let anyone know that he was in the hospital. Not his brother or my sisters or me, and especially not his colleagues. He didn't want the flowers or the visits or the phone calls. He said they wouldn't be sincere. My parents talked. He agreed to hire a carpenter to help finish the house. He said their twenty-eight years together had been the best years of his life. And then, two days later, alone in his hospital room, he had another heart attack, a massive one. He wasn't able to call for help, but it wouldn't have mattered.

I was angry at my father for keeping his hospitalization a secret, and angry at my mother for going along with his demand, but after I thought about it I concluded that for me it was best that way. My relationship with him had improved somewhat in the last few years—a recent phone conversation had been good-natured—but there would have been no bedside outpouring of forgiveness from either of us, no smiles below tear-glistened cheeks. I think it would have been very awkward. My mother showed me his wobbly handwriting on a check he'd written after the first heart attack, and I didn't want to see any more. He'd been vital and fit all his life, and that was the way I wanted to remember him.

My mother never imagined that my father would die at sixty two, that they would never live together in the Fickle Hilton when it was finally complete. But she'd always been proud of her *sisu*, that combination of courage, stoicism and blockheadedness that bolstered her Finnish forebears against harsh winters and the Soviet army. She hired two carpenters at ten dollars an hour and they finished the construction in less than a year. *They're hippies,* she would say fondly. She kidded them about their ponytails and their long beards and their tattered jeans that were held up—barely—by suspenders. They were good, honest workmen who respected all but the most impractical of my father's singular ideas about design. When their work was complete, four professors— men my father sadly believed would have come to his hospital room only for the sake of propriety—donated many hours of their time. Art Stegeman made custom cabinetry for the kitchen. Dick Genelly did the plumbing and Ed Steele did the wiring. Wynn Chase assembled a fireplace big enough to hold its own in the barn of a living room. Together, they finished the work my father had begun fifteen years before.

Four thousand square feet is a lot of space for one person, so my mother rented the downstairs to a young couple, both students at what had become Humboldt State University. She put my father's handmade desk, his typewriter and all his books in the smallest of the upstairs bedrooms. She moved into the largest one, and the other two became guest rooms. There were baseboard heaters throughout the house, but they were grossly inefficient, so she kept a fire going in the stove most of the year. It could be chilly in the unheated back rooms—fifty degrees was not uncommon during the winter—but my mother just cranked up her electric blanket a notch. I figured that if I could survive a backpack trip at 10,000 feet in October, I could deal with a few shivering trips to the bathroom, but my sisters were aghast. Mom's Refrigerated Bathrooms became Topic A at every Christmas get together.

My mother had always been interested in world history and wanted to see some of the places she'd read about, but my father seemed content to explore the local back roads, and, besides, it would have been costly for the two of them to travel abroad. Now, thanks to my father's pension and the life insurance, she could afford to travel with friends. So she went to China and Europe and

Africa, and visited relatives in Finland several times. She returned from each trip laden with mementos—wooden carvings, hand woven rugs, a spinning wheel, a teapot— and each one went on a shelf or a table or on the floor. This was not a revolving collection, but a steady accumulation. And for every piece she brought back from Guilin or Tanzania, there had to be at least a dozen she'd found at the Salvation Army or in an antique store on the Oregon coast. And that's not counting all the treasures she'd kept in boxes for years until there was enough house to display them in. Or her habit of framing things and hanging them on the walls—her paintings, other people's paintings, family photographs, photographs from her travels, photographs from my travels, Oriental prints. It was unthinkable that she would run out of places to put things. She could always crowd everything together to make room for one more, or put smaller items into bigger ones, or on top of them. Or buy another table.

Each time I went to see my mother, I would give her a hug, pet the dog, put my duffel bag in the chilly north guest bedroom and then look around to see what she'd added since my last visit. I got to be pretty good at it. "Ha! That cloisonné vase is new, isn't it, Ma? And the samovar, where did that come from?"

Her standard response was, "They wanted seventy-five dollars, but I got it for fifty. The price is on the bottom, and when my time comes, you kids make sure you get fair value."

I teased my mother about the gradual evolution of her house into a sort of museum, but I liked it because I saw how much pleasure it gave her, and because it was such a dense and personal environment. There had been plenty of things about my father's it-doesn't-matter-what-other-people-do upbringing that set my teeth on edge, but I had always been comfortable with the unusual character of our home.

Sometimes I wondered just how many artifacts my mother had amassed over the years, but I'd never got beyond counting a few groupings—the nine copper teakettles on top of the kitchen cabinets, the thirty nine trivets on the wall above the stove, the twenty five framed images in the guest bathroom. But during one of my last visits, I decided to take inventory. My mother was a night owl—she didn't totter out of her bedroom until well past noon—so I had an unhurried morning to conduct my survey. I built a fire, let the cats out, ate a bowl of cereal and then sat with a pad of paper in her chair in the living room. She spent almost all of her waking hours in that chair—her control center—often with a sleeping cat in her lap. Compared to the rest of the living room, which had a certain dust-layered formality, the chair and its immediate surroundings were a mess. Years before, she had draped a murky green bedspread over the chair, and cat fur had been accumulating on it ever since. An ottoman peeked out from beneath weeks-old sections of the *Humboldt Times Standard*, with the current week's TV schedule on top. She would toss newspapers over her head after she'd read them, so there was another haphazard pile behind her. A television—it had to be the smallest one Sony ever made—perched on an antique piano stool. A portable radio was wedged into the bracing next to the window so she could listen to her favorite talk shows and keep her doctor up to speed on Dr. Dean Edell's latest recommendations.

There was a tiered end table next to the chair. She kept her cordless phone there, along with her reading glasses, a magnifying glass, a tube of Carmex, toothpicks, and nine DayGlo pens from Mad River Community Hospital. Literally hundreds of other items, most caught in archeological limbo, were piled on the table or stuffed into little baskets and boxes. A clipping: Are You Poisoning Your Pet? A Queen of Sheba nail file. A suitcase tag from the Ching Chiang Hotel in Shanghai.

I could see most of the living room from her chair, but I had to crane my neck to see the Steinway baby grand my father bought for me in the vain hope it would facilitate a career as a pianist. That's where my mother displayed the Christmas cards each year, tucking them in among three vases of red paper roses, six ivory figurines, seven framed photographs of kids and grandkids, two ginger jars, an animal-horn jewelry box, a pair of candle holders and two jade bowls. On the wall behind the piano there were, in part, thirteen more Chinese plates, a furled gold fan, a monochromatic blue seascape on raw canvas, a framed collage of dried leaves and a hand-painted German zither.

The rest of the living room—and the house, for that matter—had the same dense texture, though the particulars varied. Except for the twenty-six Chinese mud men next to the front door, the Asian influence eventually petered out and was replaced by brass and copper vessels from the Middle East. There were clusters of antique furniture throughout the oversized living room: a couch and side chairs, a love seat, more side chairs and a couple of rockers, and all of them had attracted end tables which were nearly hidden by cloisonné and bronze. All the windows along the south wall had narrow shelves displaying what must have been close to a hundred colored glass objects—bottles and goblets and plates of cobalt, ruby, pink, amber and a half dozen shades of green. This may have been the most striking feature in the room, especially when the morning sun backlit the whole array through the leaves of a Japanese maple my father had planted many years before.

The open meadows above the house gradually became forest, and the trees around it grew and filled in so that only a small part of Eureka and the ocean beyond were still visible to the west. The driveway became a tunnel beneath interfingering branches. The outside of the house was gray with a film of undisturbed dust. Sections of the wooden stairs and handrails that led from the driveway to the back door had rotted through. Some of the crumbling boards had been replaced. Some hadn't. These changes occurred gradually over many years, and my mother had become increasingly oblivious to them. I saw the changes intermittently, and I thought back to when the land was, as I preferred it, more open to the sun. But it wasn't my home and it never really had been.

The forest's slow covering over was the fog-dampened counterpart to my mother's slow folding in. She'd always loved the trees outside her window—the redwoods especially, the supple way their wing-like branches yielded to the wind. I imagined those soft green limbs growing closer and denser. They would curve around her and coddle her tightly but gently until she disappeared altogether.

Let's Suppose

Suppose that a paint store
Exploded in space,
And splattered new colors
All over the place.

Suppose that your grandma's
Pajamas were red.
Suppose that her peepers
Were purple instead.

Imagine your sister
With tangerine ears.
Do you think if she cried
She'd shed indigo tears?

Imagine a leopard
With lavender spots.
Or turquoise begonias
In lavender pots.

Suppose that your toes
Were chartreuse in between;

That oranges were yellow
And bluebirds were green.

Imagine a rainbow
In six shades of grey;
Would your smile be as wide
If you saw that way?

Suppose that a paint store
Exploded in space.
Should we cover the earth
With a drop cloth in case?

AT THE END

OUR MOTHER DIED AT TWO O'CLOCK on a sunny Thursday afternoon. Kath was running errands, and Judy and I were stretched out on a second bed in Mad River Community Hospital's End of Life Room, sharing family stories. An hour before, our mother's frail chest had been heaving nearly fifty times a minute, but morphine had slowed her breathing, and it was now inaudible across the room. She lay on her side with her back to us, and we could see the rise and fall of the sleeve on her hospital gown.

We glanced in her direction often as we talked, and we'd done a lot of talking since we gathered at her bedside after her strokes Monday night. It had been many years since my sisters and I had spent time together away from jobs and spouses and children. We had been told that familiar voices might be comforting to our mother, and we hoped this was true.

The sleeve had stopped moving. I went for a nurse, but our mother's face had already taken on the sheen of candle wax. The nurse arrived. She bent over and placed her stethoscope deferentially on our mother's chest. She moved a little, her eyes closed in concentration. Then she straightened and shook her head.

Our mother adored cats, and she'd always had one or two, often a loosely matched pair. There had been two orange ones during our years in Seattle, two long-lived white ones, and most recently two black bruisers she called Pixie and Dixie. Kath has wondered more than once whether our mother loved her cats more than her children. Who knows, but we'd be on solid ground if we argued that she found them more entertaining. And it wasn't just cats. When an alligator lizard wandered into the house, she put it in an empty margarine tub with cuisine she judged appropriate. Regrettably, it died of apparent malnutrition. Whenever a bird, tipsy from fermented pyracantha berries, smacked into one of the picture windows, she hurried outside to cup it in her hands until it had warmed enough to fly away. Or, if the collision had been fatal, she put it in another margarine tub and stored it in the freezer for one of my father's Humboldt State colleagues who was studying avian parasites. You had to pay attention when you opened the freezer door.

Having grown up a witness to these events, it occurred to me years later that a tarantula might make a thoughtful Christmas gift for our mother. So, a day before Kath and I drove to Arcata for a holiday visit, I bought a Mexican redleg at an exotic pet store and carried it home in a Chinese restaurant take-out box. Tarantulas are cold-blooded, so Kath held the box in her lap during the five-hour drive.

Our mother was flummoxed at first. *What will I feed it?* she wanted to know. Happily, there was a pet store two doors down from Safeway that sold crickets for a nickel apiece. She named her tarantula Susie, bought a terrarium and a *Care and Feeding* pamphlet, and learned that she was more likely to be irritated by the hairs on Susie's abdomen than to lose a finger if she got fanged. Susie outgrew her exoskeleton twice over the years and our mother stayed up half the night each time to watch. She displayed the discarded skins—which looked surprisingly like their former owner—on a shelf next to a grouping of bleached rodent skulls.

Our mother's last few years traced a long declining arc. She had traveled abroad into her seventies, and after that she flew to Hawaii and Massachusetts and San Francisco to visit my sisters and me, but in time she stopped flying altogether. She handed the car keys to her caregiver and only left the house for doctors' appointments, and then only when she had the energy. Her arthritis and spinal stenosis continued to worsen, and age-addled nerves in her legs pained her. She shuffled from her well-worn chair to the kitchen or the bathroom, gasping with each step. Her dry skin itched constantly, and she raked it with yellowed fingernails. One of her front teeth had fallen out, and other teeth were loose. Wild strands of thin white hair wreathed her head like the branches of a dead oak. "Oh, God," she would say, "I look awful." Then she'd laugh.

She stopped laughing the week before she went into the hospital. She had been eating little, mostly Kit Kat bars. Sleep was difficult. She began taking an herbal remedy to soothe the torment of her itching, and it caused violent diarrhea. Her caregiver drove her to the hospital three times to rehydrate. She was admitted the third time for tests, and held for observation over the weekend.

Kath called Monday afternoon to let me know that our mother had had a seizure at the hospital. I told her I would drive to Arcata the following morning, but shortly after midnight I got a call from a family friend at the hospital, who told me that our mother had had three strokes in two hours. She urged me to get on the road as soon as possible. I packed a few clothes, stopped at 7 Eleven for a jumbo Diet Coke and headed north.

Every Monday and Friday morning while Kath and I were getting ready for school, our mother cooked hot cereal. On Tuesdays and Thursdays it was poached eggs on toast, and on Wednesday the eggs were scrambled. She packed our lunches while we ate, and as soon as we left the house she went back to bed. Dinner was nearly as predictable. We survived generic fish sticks and chicken pot pies knowing that more appealing fare would usually follow: chuck roast seasoned with powdered onion soup and baked in sealed tin foil, a polite lamb curry, and sukiyaki complete with canned bamboo shoots. For years, Wednesday was chicken night because our father, who didn't like chicken, would be on campus teaching a refresher course to high school math teachers. The chicken was always broiled with paprika and our mother always claimed both thighs and the gizzard.

She reminded us often enough that she'd grown up during the Depression. "I remember when milk was eight cents a quart," she would say, as if it still might be if only she knew where to look. She clipped coupons and saved S&H green stamps. She'd buy four loaves of day-old Safeway balloon bread for a dollar and put three of them in the freezer with the tub-entombed birds. Other kids at school—whose mothers had presumably grown up during the Depression, too—ate roast beef sandwiches with crisps of lettuce curling out just as they did in the Campbell's ads in the *Saturday Evening Post*. We got baloney and cheese sandwiches and a daily allotment of stale Busy Baker ginger snaps from a two pound bag.

In fairness, Christmas was different. Our mother followed Grandma Klose's recipes for pfeffernüsse and rum balls dusted with powdered sugar. She also baked reindeer-shaped butter cookies sprinkled with red and green sugar crystals. She put so much candied fruit in her fruitcake that everyone else's seemed grainy and dry. The turkey was always cooked just right, and her stuffing and giblet gravy were beyond words. "Your grandmother's was better," she'd say.

The eastern sky was brightening as I drove into the hospital parking lot. I walked in not knowing whether my mother was alive, and I wasn't sure how to ask about her at the nurse station. But she was lying in one of the two beds in Room 114, her eyes closed and her mouth agape as it often was when she was napping in her chair. With Kath's firm insistence, she had finally parted company with her marginally competent general practitioner, so I didn't know the doctor who came by on his rounds at 7:00am. He yelled "Hey, Rachel" in my mother's face, and she gave him a wild look and grunted. She had already begun to move her left arm, but her left leg was limp when he hefted it.

Kath arrived mid-afternoon from Boston, and Judy flew in from Honolulu a few hours later. She'd brought a lei of tuberoses and red carnations, and I hung it on the IV stand. Judy said *Hmm* and moved it to our mother's pillow in case she could smell the fragrance. She was on Dilantin to prevent more seizures, and Ativan for sedation. She seemed to sleep relatively peacefully when the Ativan was at full force, but as it wore off she became restless, scratching herself and moaning. We thought one of the medicines might be aggravating her itching and asked if anything could be done, but there was already Benadryl in her IV, and she couldn't take an oral antihistamine because the strokes had left her at least temporarily unable to swallow. She tried to speak, and though most of her words were croaks, she repeated them often enough that we could understand some of what she was trying to tell us. She wanted talcum powder for the itching. Kath helped her with the container, and she dumped a generous amount between her breasts and spread it over her skin. It didn't help.

She was thirsty, and she wanted some Mountain Dew. Kath leaned over the bed and spoke quietly in her ear. "You can't drink anything yet because of what happened to you."

"But I want some Mountain Dew."

"I know you do, Mom, but it might make you choke."

"But I'm thirsty." Kath looked up at Judy and me with tears rolling down her cheeks. Judy and I cried because we couldn't stop the thirst or the itching, and because we knew how much our sister wanted her mother to live forever.

The doctor gave us an unhopeful prognosis. Based on conversations we'd had with our mother over the years, Judy and I wanted him to withhold intervention. Kath disagreed at first, but we all knew there could be no happy ending. Our mother would probably survive the strokes, but after many years of shunning any form of exercise on principle, she would be a poor candidate for rehabilitation. She'd lived for decades with her pets as her only companions, and she was fiercely opposed to leaving her home for any kind of managed care. Round the clock nursing at home might have been feasible, but for what purpose? Our mother had been uncharacteristically depressed the week before she went into the hospital, and we hadn't told her yet about the strokes.

On Wednesday morning, the doctor ordered a chest X-ray and blood tests. Our mother was showing signs of a urinary tract infection, and something was happening in her lungs, possibly pneumonia. A nurse was having a hard time inserting a needle for a blood draw. Our mother struggled and cried out. Judy tried to hold her arm steady, surprised by how much strength she still had. Kath was anguished. "Why are you doing this?" she asked.

I left the room to talk with a social worker. While I was away, our mother spoke. "Let me die," she said. "Just let me die."

Before I was old enough to name them, I'd noticed the vaguely disquieting colors our mother had chosen for the drapes, the upholstered furniture and the rugs in our home in Seattle: burgundy, tainted yellow, brooding greens. Her palette brightened a bit in Arcata, but after my father died she redecorated, and her favorite colors were now just two, pale aquamarine and olive green. She wore these colors. She sat on them. She slept in them. Soon after my parents married, my father encouraged her to develop her talent as a watercolorist, and the early still lifes and dockside scenes of fishing boats she hung in the dining room were daubed with red and gold and violet. But her later, gestural landscapes were all blues and greens save for a barn or a golden California hillside. Now, so were the carpet, the drapes, the hand towels in the guest bathroom, and—why not?—the toilet paper.

For years, I'd eaten off a set of Heath stoneware I bought at a garage sale for a song. I'd been seduced less by the colors than by the lineage and the price, but each time my mother came for a visit, she commented on the pale blue glaze. Finally, she proposed a trade. She'd take the stoneware and I'd get the simple but handsome flatware our family had grown up with. She offered to throw in a set of blue-green dinner plates, but I'd recently been to Pier 1 Imports and was thinking more along the lines of fire engine red.

The doctor met with us at noon. The X-ray and the blood tests were inconclusive, but a urinary tract infection and pneumonia were likely. These were conditions he could treat, problems he could solve. But Kath now agreed with Judy and me that our mother should be allowed to die, as comfortably as possible. Reluctantly, the doctor agreed to withhold intervention, to disconnect the oxygen and the fluid IV, and to administer morphine as well as Ativan. My sisters and I traded looks. We were certain— almost—that we had made the right decision.

The End of Life Room, which the med-surg nurses had decorated at their own expense, was at the end of a corridor. It was quieter there, with little foot traffic and no audible conversations from adjacent patient rooms.

The monitor that had beeped faithfully and discordantly each time our mother's IV line got kinked had been silenced.

Family friends Kath and I had known since childhood dropped by with an armload of take-out Mexican food from Hey Juan. We ate and talked about our respective mothers, who had been close friends. We shared bits of family history and traded bear stories. We laughed and chuckled and brushed away tears.

Our family had been introduced to beachcombing soon after we arrived in Arcata. Charlie Moon, a music professor who would soon be my new piano teacher, was a serious rock hound, and he took us to an ocean beach north of Arcata to introduce us to his passion. There were intermittent patches of gravel strewn along the gently curved beach, and Charlie showed us what to look for. Pale agates, bright red and yellow pieces of jasper, and two kinds of jade—dark green nephrite, and chloromelanite, which could be almost black.

We spread out along the beach to scrutinize countless small stones and pebbles, and Charlie periodically called us back together. "Look at this," he would say. "This is jade." Our mother would counter with a few pieces she'd picked up, and he would give them a quick glance and shake his head. "No. No, that's not it." They had this conversation several times over the course of the afternoon. Finally, our mother said, "Oh, I see. If you find it, it's jade. If I find it, it's not."

Despite her inauspicious debut, our mother soon learned to spot the one stone among thousands that might be jade, and she came to relish the search just as Charlie did. She would spend an afternoon at the beach once a week or so, sometimes with Kath and me, or with a friend, or by herself. She wore the same scruffy outfit for years: black rubber boots, a long suede coat, and a baggy pair of pants that were—yes—an awful shade of green. She had a big red bucket, and, if she was alone, the holstered .22 revolver that my father insisted she carry.

She sometimes did her looking at the edge of the surf, which, she reasoned, would be tossing up stones she'd see before anyone else. She moved generally from one patch of gravel to the next, veering opportunistically toward a particular color or glint. She directed part of her consciousness to the oncoming waves, occasionally dashing to higher ground to keep her feet dry. You might think, seeing the zigzag of her footprints in the sand, that she had been drinking.

The bucket got heavier with each stone she added for later assessment, and she could be lugging ten pounds or more by the time she got back to the car. After dinner, she would sit in her chair by one of the living room windows to sort through the day's harvest. Any agates she had found she would toss a bit dismissively into a wicker basket on the floor. Then, one at a time, she inspected the remaining stones, setting aside the jade and dumping the many also-rans back into the red bucket. She brought up the sheen on the piees of jade by rubbing them over the oily skin next to her nose.

The next day, she upended the bucket over a sort of midden on the far side of a redwood stump across the creek from the house. Someday, perhaps, an archeologist will puzzle over this pile of orphaned rock. Or, better, someone will load it into the back of a pickup truck, haul it out to the coast, and throw it back on the beach.

Our mother dressed carelessly in her last years, wearing the same cat-fur upholstered housecoat for months. But she still liked to display her jewelry, and she entered the hospital with six rings on her fingers. A nurse's aide helped my sisters remove five of them with Vaseline, but the sixth was caught behind an arthritic knuckle and wouldn't budge. A specialist was called in, a plump nurse with orange hair. She raised the bed to a suitable height and began wrapping the finger in question with a length of what looked like thick dental floss. It took several tries and some firm tugging, but the ring eventually came off, and she handed it to one of my sisters. She placed our mother's withered arm back across her chest. "There you go, Pumpkin," she said. She pushed a button to lower the bed. "Going down," she said, and she turned and walked from the room.

gnaB giB

I.

Many years ago (before baseball)
All God's universe
Went blooey from a tiny speck.

Be a bit of a chore
To stuff it all back.

II.

Start with easy things
Like Belgian waffles and
Management seminars and
Gluten-free yogurt.

Be systematic. Make a list:
Anchovies
Automatic transmissions
Sandra Bullock
The Sahara Desert
Thumbtacks

Hire a consultant.

Get everything together in one place.
Put little things inside of big things.
Put big things inside a really big thing
And jump up and down on the lid.

Whew.

III.

Oh, damn!
Forgot Amerigo Vespucci.

Shots Were Fired

When our cat Stubby died at nineteen, my father built a casket from kiln-dried redwood and laid him inside on an unopened copy of the Sunday *Chronicle*, because he liked to sleep on newspapers. Years later, the brown and white mutt we'd had since I was ten was dying of cancer. When her suffering became too hard to witness, my father carried her gently into the woods and shot her. My mother said he should have acted a day or two sooner, and I imagine he knew that, but it would have been very difficult for him, even in such circumstances, to kill another sentient being. When I think about how much my parents loved animals, how each of them sentimentalized our family pets in different ways, I continue to be surprised that they allowed me to own several weapons, knowing that I could—and did—use them to kill.

Like many boys of a certain age, I was fascinated by violence and death, but I was also compassionate. I toasted ants with a magnifying glass and then raged at one of my friends when he shot a garter snake with his BB gun.

I had always wanted a pair of holstered cap guns and a kid-sized Stetson, but I never got them. What I did get, when I was old enough, was a BB gun of my own, a Daisy air rifle I'd coveted since I first saw it advertised in *Boy's Life*. The metal parts were blue and the plastic parts were white, a color palette better suited to Annie Oakley, but those were the colors I wanted.

After I opened my first container of BBs and rolled a handful of them into the tube below the barrel of my new weapon, I needed targets, and I was pretty sure Roy Rogers would never *plunk at tin cans*. I'd seen rats in the sagging garage next door, but they were as shrewd as they were repulsive, and they didn't show themselves as casually after I'd fired a few shots at them. Besides, there could be no closure without a confirmed body count, and I wasn't inclined to look for dead rats in dark corners where there could be live ones.

So I shot birds instead. Oregon juncos, mostly, because there were lot of them near our house and it was easy to approach within shooting range. Our land-lord raised furbearing animals called nutria—big rats, as far as I was concerned—in concrete pens not far from the garage. The juncos hung out at the pens to help themselves to spilled feed, and I ambushed them there. A BB gun is not a precise weapon, and I was a poor marksman, so I missed most of the time. When I didn't miss, the bird would fall limply to the ground, its head lolling at an odd angle. I would be ashamed that I had taken the life of an animal so small and powerless, and yet I knew I would come back because I couldn't resist the urge to hunt. My mother must have wept at the thought of my murderous behavior, but she didn't confront me, believing perhaps that no child of hers could practice such evil for very long.

My cousin Bob once brought a Wham-O slingshot with him when his family came north for a visit. It was a simple but powerful weapon, and after seeing it in action I immediately bought one of my own. The gravel on our driveway served as my ammunition. The harder I pulled back on the rubber straps, the faster and farther the stones would fly. I launched them one after another toward old redwood stumps, watching them whack against the wood, and scrambling to the side when one of them ricocheted straight back.

It was inevitable, once I'd become reasonably accurate, that I would stalk the juncos again. I gathered a pocketful of the roundest marble-sized stones I could find and headed for the nutria pens. I had become a better shot than I imagined, and the results were appallingly spectacular, a sudden burst of grey and white feathers that hung in the air for an instant and then drifted down like snowflakes. This time my shame prevailed.

I made a David and Goliath sling from two leather shoelaces and a leather pocket cut from the tongue of an old work boot. With it, I could hurl a stone the size of a golf ball, and it would thrum like a bullet on the way to my new target, a blackened redwood snag with nothing breakable behind it. The snag was about thirty feet high, with two holes near the top that looked like ghost eyes. One of my ambitions in life at the time was to sling a stone through one of those holes.

Guns and hunting were part of the culture in Humboldt County, and, in fact, my father had bought a *sporterized* World War I Chilean army rifle from Sears Roebuck to assassinate the deer that periodically chewed my mother's flowers to the ground. He never fired a shot at one of them—we would have been shocked if he had—but he and I did set out some bottles and cans to see how the thing worked.

I'd heard some of my classmates talk about guns often enough that I could speak basic *Field and Stream*. I recognized a Winchester Model 94 when I saw one on the gun rack in the back window of a pickup truck. I knew the difference between center fire and rim fire. Ditto between bolt action, lever action and pump. I thought I ought to have a rifle of my own, and darned if my father didn't agree, when I was twelve, that I could.

We comparison-shopped for .22s and I chose a bolt action Remington. He told me how to carry it and where not to point it, and he enrolled me in an NRA Safe Hunter course. He offered no advice about what to shoot.

I took my rifle with me on our last trip to Pear Point. I planned to hunt rabbits, which, unlike juncos, we could barbeque. I shot at two or three, and they flinched as the bullets whined overhead. Then I winged one. I ran to where the rabbit lay on its side, uselessly pumping its hind legs. Its eyes were gleaming with pain and fear. I broke its neck with the butt of my rifle, wiped the tears from my cheeks and carried the rabbit back to camp for dinner. I've never hunted since.

An Ode to Piracy

Note: Dorothy Parker wrote a remarkably similar poem,
Song of Perfect Propriety, which I must have seen
many years before I wrote this one.

I wish I'd been a pirate on a pirate ship at night
Swilling rum and belching in the golden cabin light
Clad in tattered pirate garb, stiff with sweat and worse
Joining sotted singing fests of Rabelaisian verse.
Oh, I wish I'd been a pirate.

Suppose I'd been a pirate with a pirate's eye for gold
Storing rival pirates in a dank and fetid hold
Antagonist of sordid tales of pillaging and rape
Told by simple village folk with simple mouths agape.
Oh, I wish I'd been a pirate.

Let's say I had a misanthropic pirate point of view
And missing limbs, if possible, though missing teeth
   would do
And several scurvy cabin mates with whom to sit
   and dine
Washing down a flyblown feast with sour dregs of wine.
Oh, I wish I'd been a pirate.

Ah, to dangle maidens over shark-infested seas
Negotiating social favors, heedless of their pleas
To chase a coy companion fore and aft about the deck
Posing pointed questions with a cutlass to the neck.
Oh, I wish I'd been a pirate.

To search for buried treasure on a fog-enshrouded coast
Digging deep in tidal seep, transcendently engrossed
And when the moldy chest is struck and opened to the air
To curse the moldy pirate hoard disintegrating there.
Oh, I wish I'd been a pirate.

To while away a sultry Caribbean afternoon
Crushing lice and dozing by an emerald lagoon
Drifting into reverie with filthy beard achest
Contemplating pirate deeds unspeakable at best.
Oh, whate'er became of pirates?

I wish I were a pirate on a vast uncharted sea
Horizon-bound on billowed sails, no better place to be
No scheduled stops, no nelly fops, no civil dentistry
...Hmm
If not for seasick tendencies, I'd sure a pirate be.
I turn a ghastly shade of green, or I'd a pirate be.

A Brief History of Inhalation

I INHALED, BILL. SEVERAL TIMES. These lapses of judgment have left me spiritually adrift, motivationally challenged and morally bankrupt. I've never been impeached, though.

The trouble began, as trouble often did in the late '60s, in Looney Tunes Berkeley, self-appointed political conscience to the galaxy. As a raw freshman, I had moved into Ehrman Hall, one of twelve eight story dormitories that still loom over the houses and apartments of South Campus. These dorms were as homey as upended ice trays, so many freshmen like me trod a well-worn path past The East is Red bookstore to Telegraph Avenue. We savored the brute fragrance of patchouli oil as we shopped for patterned madras bedspreads that we would billow from the ceiling or hang as partitions or even use to cover a bed. Put the bedspreads together with paper light globes from Japan, crude brass bells from India and sprays of sandalwood incense and—voila—our rooms were personalized.

A few of my high school classmates—the ones who grocked Country Joe and the Fish and drove from Arcata to the Haight-Ashbury to check out the scene—spoke knowingly about getting stoned, but I didn't see my first joint until Ehrman Hall. The doors along the narrow hallway that linked our dozen rooms were often open, especially in the evenings. If one of them was closed, it might mean that the occupants were studying or sleeping or—conceivably—that somebody had gotten lucky with a coed who'd sneaked up the fire stair. But if you could smell a sweet stink drifting into the hallway, and especially if you could also hear the drone of a sitar, then someone was smoking pot. And if you could hear a sitar but couldn't smell anything, then someone had probably stuffed a wet towel up against the gap at the bottom of the door. This was an unnecessary precaution in Berkeley in 1967, but I liked the boys-in-the-secret-clubhouse aura, and wanted to be a part of it. In time I was.

My first inhalation, followed immediately by my first fit of goggle-eyed coughing, took place not in one of our rooms but on the roof, where several of my dormmates and I had gone to share a joint and peer into the windows of the women's dorm across the courtyard. It was an unrewarding evening on both counts, but a few weeks later I felt a pleasant thick-headedness after several of us shared a joint during a late night amble down Telegraph to the International House of Pancakes. I didn't giggle or see God, but I'd been told that it took practice to recognize the effects.

During my sophomore year, in order to keep our

shares of the rent at a manageable sixty dollars a month, two dormmates, Will and Henry, and Henry's friend Junior and I moved into a generic two bedroom apartment half a block from Ehrman Hall. Junior, as adventurous as he was sly, took responsibility for maintaining our collective stash. One afternoon he served as our negotiator as we sat in the living room with two overdressed "brothers" from West Oakland, reviewing the terms and conditions of a modest investment in what we were repeatedly assured was Michoacán's finest, as if any of us were about to examine it closely and say, *Are you sure this isn't Zacatecas Purple?* Whatever it was, it cost ten dollars a lid and came in a baggy rolled to the diameter of a ballpark frank. We figured a lid to be good for about thirty joints, depending on who was doing the rolling. But this was well before Maui Wowie and China Creek Skunk Weed, before single plants were coddled like hothouse orchids, before everything except the buds was worth little more than barn sweepings. It took skill then to roll a functional joint, to keep the bits of stem parallel to the length of it so that they wouldn't poke holes in the Zig Zag paper and prevent the thing from drawing properly. Licorice-flavored rolling papers became popular, not because of the taste but because they were more durable and puncture-resistant.

Junior had a rolling machine, a simple device with a miniature red conveyor belt looped around two rollers. It turned out magnificent, firmly packed joints, but we didn't use it much because it diluted our kinship with jazz musicians in porkpie hats. Either way, at least two of us got together before we fired up a joint. Passing it back and forth was a bonding experience, and—equally important—one of us would be free to chase down exploding seeds and flick them into an ashtray before they scorched the landlord's carpet.

We typically smoked a joint or two after dinner on Friday night. We moved Will's stereo speakers out from the wall and aimed them at each other so that when we lay down on the floor between them, they served as a pair of communal headphones. We cued up our favorite stoner music, turned off the lights, propped up our heads on pillows, closed our eyes and watched the show. We were particularly fond of Blood, Sweat and Tears' *Child is Father to the Man*, Jefferson Airplane's *Crown of Creation* and Santana's eponymous first album.

It's a commonplace that getting stoned makes you more of who you already are, and if this is true, Bill Clinton was wise not to inhale—he might have exploded. As an introvert, I risked the obverse possibility of disappearing altogether, and my most engrossing pot-propelled adventures took place entirely within my head. Our Friday night ritual, nominally social but essentially solitary, was an ideal setting for my immersion in self, and in music. I was happily prone to synesthesia, to seeing music as a sort of screensaver of pulsing and oozing colors on the insides of my eyelids. A searing cat-on-the-back-fence guitar lick became a spiky yellow electrocardiogram. A bass riff bounded left to right like a DayGlo chrysanthemum. Could I drive safely in such a state? Write a term paper? Take a call from my mother? Who knows? What I could do, I found, was focus effortlessly on a single component of the music. I could snake into all those carefully mixed and balanced layers to pull out a rhythm track or a backing vocal.

After I graduated from college I began listening to classical music while stoned, and the imagery I saw, like the music itself, was more majestic than what I'd seen while listening to rock 'n' roll. I was glued spread-eagled to the hull of the Starship Enterprise, moving at warp 9 and not moving at all as a solemn procession of galaxies and black holes wheeled below me.

I found that this pot-sharpened focus supplemented my twelve years of piano lessons and the music history classes I'd taken at Berkeley to help me discern the melodic structure of an orchestral work. I was wary at first, mindful of the gleefully recounted stories we'd all heard about acidheads who jotted down profound insights as they tripped, only to find their jottings unintelligible the next day. But the melodies of Tchaikovsky's *Serenade for Strings*, which I perceived while stoned to be dancing around the C major scale— descending in the first movement, ascending in the second and third, and counterpoised but ultimately descending in the fourth—continued to dance in this way when I listened again with a clear head. (What was different was that I didn't wonder how many other people on the planet were listening to Tchaikovsky at the same time, and, of those, how many were stoned.)

Henry and Junior augmented the music they heard in their own ways, staring at black light posters and candle flames, flipping a light switch on and off, and playing flashlight beams across each other's closed eyes. (Will was usually in Stockton with his girlfriend for the weekend.) All of us succumbed to the munchies if we'd had the foresight to lay in a supply of cookies and ice cream. Henry was the least disciplined, once eating an entire package of Chips Ahoy and then, shortly thereafter, literally tossing his cookies.

Will, who studied a good deal more than the rest of us, graduated cum laude in the spring and went off to law school. Henry, Junior and I continued on as roommates the next fall, joined by Rolf, a former dormmate who meditated and ate yogurt. The four of us squeezed into a well-worn one bedroom apartment just off Shattuck Avenue which came equipped with cockroaches and an unobstructed view of the Chevron station next door. Henry, who'd found the place, laid claim to part of the original living room. Jimmy and I shared the bedroom, now accessible only through the bathroom by way of the kitchen. Rolf slept in a walk-in closet.

We were by now sophisticated drug users who would happily spend twenty dollars for a lid of alleged Panama Red, and we had *paraphernalia*—a little Bilbo Baggins pipe with a wire mesh screen in the bowl, roach clips, and bongs cunningly fashioned by poking a joint-sized hole near one end of the cardboard tube from a roll of paper towels. Our group inhalations were less formal but no less distracting than they'd been the year before. Between dope and Revolution in the Streets, I struggle to remember how we found the time—or the discipline—to attend classes and write term papers.

On the morning after the Selective Service System's first draft lottery, I was sitting next to my friend Bimbo in Spiro Kostov's architectural history class. Professor K. was the rare lecturer who could induce undergraduates to stay awake for flying buttresses, but on this day even he couldn't hold our attention. Bimbo and I compared notes and discovered that we'd each drawn numbers—mine was 48—that guaranteed travel to Vietnam when our student deferments expired. *Only one thing to do*, said Bimbo. We eased quietly into an aisle and out of the lecture hall and then walked to a nearby apartment, where several of Bimbo's friends were sitting cross-legged around a hookah, the first I'd seen. *Even Junior would be impressed*, I thought, as Bimbo made brief introductions. Someone put a match to the brass receptacle above the water bowl, and the serpent-like tube began circulating. When it came to me, I took a confident pull, felt nothing and exhaled a prodigious cloud of smoke that brought quick laughter. Ten minutes later I was higher than I'd ever been, amazed at how easily I could take in the smoke without coughing.

I don't remember much about the rest of the day, but, for whatever purpose, we returned to campus and wandered downstream along the tree-shaded banks of Strawberry Creek. It was an unremarkable activity and I recognized it as such, but it was different, too, as though the sunlight had become bright buzzing Jell-O in which we were gently immersed. We were spies, perhaps, or the first European explorers as we picked our way down the boulder-strewn creek bed. At West Gate, we stepped out into the open. I imagined that the parked cars I saw on

Oxford Street were resting animals, cows maybe. I giggled. *Do you guys think they're edible?*

I launched myself into higher orbit only once, during one of my summers as a seasonal ranger at Richardson Grove State Park, a no-hair-touching-the-collar realm considerably less forgiving than Berkeley. The fulltime rangers didn't wear sidearms then, but they creased their uniform shirts with great care, took diligent notes in their on-the-job training classes, and knew how to *recognize the distinctive odor*. The Humboldt County Sheriff's Department routinely busted nearby growers and paraded down Main Street in Garberville with ten foot plants draped ostentatiously over their SUVs even as the Deputy Sheriff's two sons—coworkers at the park—were said to rummage through the trash cans behind the substation looking for discarded evidence.

The seasonal employees at Richardson Grove were divided fairly evenly between stoners and divinity students. The former began each summer intending to be discreet, but, by August, *Wanna smoke some more dope?*—or, more efficiently, *WSSMD?*—was once again a standard greeting. We were loaded after work, loaded on night patrol, loaded as we recited campfire talks about the perils of poison oak. I say *we* rhetorically, because my own use of marijuana was by then occasional

and opportunistic, but I considered myself philosoph-
ically aligned with the potheads and therefore hipper.

Maria—A plump Latina who worked in the park
entrance station and served as living proof of Parks and
Recreation's newly discovered embrace of ethnic
diversity—had a brother doing a tour in Vietnam. He'd
sent her, somehow, a couple joints of Thai Stick, which
she graciously and after much encouragement offered to
share. A half dozen of us gathered in her cabin to fire
them up, and I'd taken four or five hits before I realized
that I'd signed on for a whole new order of magnitude. I
was on a fast rising elevator, increasingly anxious to get
off at the next floor, but there were no buttons to push,
and paranoia—the only other passenger—was crowding
my space big time. I panicked and headed straight for
the comforting familiarity of my own cabin. I turned on
the radio and lay on my bed. Watergate was nearing
vindication—Nixon would resign in a week or two—
and the impeachment hearings were being broadcast
live. These hearings were taking place on this planet, I
was sure of that, so I locked in on Roger Mudd's
professionally modulated voice, which was arcing over
an entire continent of fruited plains and purple
mountains' majesty to calm me in my hour of need. I
could see his big rubber lips extruding sentences like
toothpaste. Never had I been so purposefully engrossed

in Con-gressional Procedures. My head was still vibrating the next morning.

The dandiest thing about marijuana, I once concluded while straight, was that it effectively doubled your options in life. You could watch TV, or you could watch TV stoned. Ditto reading a book or washing the dishes. I'd long honored this principle mainly in the breach. Dope cost money, stunted incentive, made depression more depressing, and was, after all, illegal. But it had its place. Watching *Fantasia* or *Yellow Submarine* without entering the state of mind in which they were presumably created would be a comparatively pallid experience. Dope diffused the small fear of skiing EXPERTS ONLY runs with INTERMEDIATE skills. On rare occasions, it had taken lovemaking to a more sensual place. I think it did, anyway. I was stoned at the time.

Certifiably naïve, I once presented most of this line of reasoning to my father. I'd never intended to raise the issue with him, but Kath, as a freshman at UC Santa Cruz, had begun serving as our parents' inadvertent correspondent from the front lines of the drug-enhanced Sexual Revolution, and he was alarmed. He asked me— the stable one, he said—to keep an eye on her, and this enraged me. I was on her side, not his. I wanted my share of the adventure, not congratulations for watching it through a keyhole. My grades may have been respectable and my drug use modest, but my father would know that I, too, had broken the law.

I also wanted my father to understand that I smoked dope for what I considered to be rational reasons. As a mathematician, I knew that he valued rationality. Was it not rational to welcome variety into your life, to make full use of your senses? I didn't plan to offer my father a joint, didn't imagine that he would reconsider and agree with me, but I did hope he'd acknowledge that I'd given the matter some thought, *that I wasn't, like, leading an unexamined life, man*. I wanted conditional approval.

I didn't get it. I had danced adroitly—but apparently not convincingly—around the obvious, that smoking dope was, more than anything, enjoyable, and enjoyment didn't feature prominently in my father's worldview. His anhedonia wasn't all encompassing. He and my mother enjoyed, by her accounting, a satisfying sexual relationship throughout their marriage. He liked Chinese food. He clearly enjoyed music and read at least some books simply for pleasure. But he was a driven man who often talked about obligations. My twelve years of piano lessons had been his idea, not mine. My music teachers said I had potential, and my father believed that I was obliged to realize that potential so I could enrich other people's lives. He also believed that because he'd received his education essentially without cost from the University of California, he was obliged to give back by teaching at a state university. His giving was made arduous by his obsessive thoroughness. When, as a child, I walked past his study on the way to the bathroom in the small hours, I often found him slumped at his desk, snoring over a stack of lower division homework that any of his colleagues would have delegated to a teaching assistant.

My father heard me out, enduring my betrayal of his values, then directed the conversation to—of all places—Mao's China. Unaware as we all were of the Cultural Revolution then in progress, he said that the Chinese had got it about right. Their lives were simple and direct. They worshipped no false gods, especially not materialism, and they presumably didn't waste their time getting high. In the end, my father got up and walked away, a thin haze of disgust floating over the chair where he'd been sitting. It wasn't smoke.

Daphne and Simon
A Case Study

Daphne's room is very messy,
Simon's room is neat.
Simon's shoes are very dressy,
Daphne wears bare feet.

Daphne stores an extra pizza
Underneath her bed.
Simon sorts his socks by color,
Purple next to red.

Simon keeps his yellow pencils
Neatly in a row.
Daphne had a pencil once...
Wherever did it go?

Daphne stays up late at night
And often sleeps 'til noon.
Simon's up at six o'clock
To practice his bassoon.

Simon's fond of vegetables,
And always eats them first.

Daphne says they're poisonous
And spinach is the worst.

Daphne has a guinea pig,
Two bunnies and a bird.
Simon's dog is Stephanie
Persephone, III.

Daphne's room is anarchy
While Simon's is serene.
You can be like either one,
Or somewhere in between.

About My Father

HE HAD WONDERFUL, SUN-BROWNED HANDS. The tips of his fingers were rounded and full, each nail trimmed to a neat, white crescent. In photographs, he sometimes stands with his arms self-consciously posed, but my eyes are always drawn to his hands—thumbs straight down, fingers curled like parentheses.

When he sat forming thoughts at his desk, he held his fountain pen in his right hand, flexing his fingers back and forth in sequence like the legs of a galloping horse. His handwriting was very small, the *m's* and *n's* and *u's* often barely distinguishable from one another, but with every defining wiggle present and accounted for. In the classroom, he wrote in block letters on the blackboard, very fast. *Tap-t-ti-tap-t-ti-tap-tap-tap*. Very fast and straight, with all the letters the same size.

He had always wanted to learn to play the organ. He intended to build one from a kit, and why not? It was less complicated than building a house, and in fact the house he was building would have an organ-sized alcove off the living room. He began taking piano lessons from the spinster in the peeling Victorian across the street from Safeway. But by that time, arthritis had stiffened his fingers just enough to make them unmanageably clumsy at the keyboard. Perhaps he invoked for himself a favorite saying he'd said often enough to me: *Who promised you justice?* Or perhaps, like me, he thought it was a damn shame.

He wore his denim jacket when he worked outside in cool weather, which in Arcata was most of the time. An Eisenhower jacket, he would have called it. There had been two. The first one eventually became so tattered that my mother refused to wash it anymore. She threw it out and bought him another one, which I kept as a remembrance after he died. It's faded in more places than not, spattered with paint and completely frayed at the collar and cuffs. Nicely broken in.

Had my father lived to see his granddaughter growing up, he would have been amused to see the remnants of her treasured receiving blanket, so fragile that Kath bundled it with string before she washed it. Rachel might in turn be amused to know that, evening after evening, her grandfather wore his ragged denim jacket as he put away the same tools he would need the next morning, and swept up sawdust where more sawdust would soon fall.

He smelled good. Mennen Skin Bracer with an overtone of sweat when the occasion warranted. He always wore a suit to work, and never took off his coat or loosened his tie or rolled up his sleeves even as he sat grading papers late into the night. I thought he looked very distinguished, particularly after his grey hair turned an elegant silver-white. He grew a magnificent beard one summer, and it softened him. Small children called him Santa Claus, giggled and clapped their hands over their mouths, and he would grin, self-conscious and delighted. But he shaved it off before classes began in the fall so his colleagues wouldn't assume he'd drifted to the left.

He was contemptuous of academic politics and belittled the professors who spent their days leaning against the wall in each other's offices, dropping cigarette ashes on the floor and talking shop instead of counseling their students or preparing their lectures. I remember a warm afternoon when my mother and I sat with him while he was working on the roof. He, too, was talking shop that day, and at one point he described a faculty member "who couldn't find his ass with both hands, the fucking so and so …"

"Oh, Orval," my mother had burst in, half in shock, half in mock indignation. It was the only time I heard him use the f-word and I don't imagine she'd heard it often, either. He gave me a fine, sly look.

He was an explorer of sorts, and by the time he married at thirty seven, he'd seen a fair bit of the world with all his expenses paid by the Merchant Marine and then by the Army Air Force. As a family man, he stayed closer to home, driving every road in the region to see whether the country he traversed would be as he'd imagined it. These investigations were daylong family outings that began on familiar highways and continued on lesser paved and—ideally—unpaved roads until we arrived at a remote and shaded picnic spot next to a river. This accomplished, we ate our lunch and then kicked up dust and gravel until we intersected a familiar paved highway to loop back home. Once, during my college years, the two of us spent four days checking out back roads in the thinly populated counties east of Humboldt. Our conversations were few and guarded during those four days, but when we gazed at a well formed mountain ridge, I believe we were both moved in the same way.

My father believed that a good joke ought to be retold from time to time. I remember three in particular.

Housewife: We have twins, you know.
That only happens once every hundred times.
Repairman: Good heavens, ma'am.
How do you find time to do the housework?

Hostess: Can I offer you a pancake?
Guest: Oh, no. Thank you. I already have
a trunkful. Would you like to see my Howard
Johnson Blueberry?

Salesman: Good morning, ma'am.
Can I interest you in a book?
Housewife: No thanks. We already have one.

I heard the last one every time I declined his offer to buy me another book without color illustrations or pirates.

He was close to his mother and looked after her from the time my paternal grandfather died years before I was born. He wrote to her often, reassuring her from Sydney or Accra or Karachi that he was fine, verifying that she'd received a check he'd mailed her, asking about cousins and aunts. After he was married, he sent Grandma Klose many black and white photographs of our family—my mother with one of her cats, me at two or three years old sitting in a canoe, engulfed by a life jacket. *Sat the little Hiawatha*, he had written on the back.

After she broke her hip in her early 80s, his mother moved in with Uncle Alvin and Aunt Eloise in the East Bay. My father wanted to help care for her, wanted her to live with us in the house he was building, and even after she entered a nursing home he hoped to bring her up to Arcata, to rescue her from disinfected corridors and the staff who wheeled her, along with the other residents, into the dining room once a week to ring bells in time to music. When she died, it was as if he had failed her.

His middle name was M (with no period). He could whistle. He had athlete's foot. He thought June Allyson was cute as a button. He voted for the Prohibition party candidate in 1960 because he couldn't stomach Kennedy *or* Nixon. He once owned a Harley-Davidson.

He could pee straight with no hands. He taught me how to double clutch.

Daphne and Simon
A Genteel Culture War

Simon says the finer things
Ennoble and enrich.
Daphne says Monet's okay
But opera makes her itch.

Simon reads Thucydides,
De Maupassant and Poe.
Daphne feels that Danielle Steel's
A far as she could go.

Simon writes his sonnets
With a calligraphic pen.
Daphne wrote her uncle once
But can't remember when.

Simon's learned the native tongues
Of Tongans, Thais and Turks.
Daphne took a clock apart
(The clock no longer works).

Most of Simon's favorite plays
Are tales of souls accursed.

Most of Daphne's favorite plays
Are throws from third to first.

"The Bolshoi!" Simon hollers
As he flips to PBS.
Daphne's parents also watch,
To Daphne's great distress.

Simon sits enraptured
As the dancers twirl and leap.
Daphne yawns and rubs her eyes
And promptly falls asleep.

To Have and Have Not

WHEN SHE WAS THREE OR SO, my friend Steve's daughter Kate pointed a small finger at my head and said, "You don't have any hair," which was not entirely true. I responded by asking if I could borrow some of hers, and she grinned hugely. "No!"

I used to have hair, and when I was Kate's age it was Aryan blond just like hers. My mother cut it short and I didn't give it much attention. When I was older, she let it grow longer, at least on top, and I wetted my comb to shape a little crest above my forehead. I was in high school before I let it grow long enough to see that, like nearly everything about my adolescence, I didn't like it at all. It was thin and limp and no longer blond. Most of my classmates had full heads of straight hair. My hair had a flat wave that was still there each time I glanced in the mirror to see if it had somehow disappeared.

I could have asked my mother to cut it short again, but the only kid I knew who had really short hair was the son of Arcata's Presbyterian minister, and I didn't think of him as a role model. So, instead, I stopped using shampoo except on the weekends because shampoo made my waves wavier. Washing without shampoo gave me some grease to work with, especially at the end of the week. I could plaster my hair against my scalp and it would be more or less straight until it got close to my ears.

When I set off to college, I intended to grow my hair down to my shoulders so people would think I was getting laid by girls who didn't wear panties. But I wanted hair like Gregg Allman, not Jerry Garcia, so I began using a styling gel called Dippity-do. I was too self-conscious to buy it myself, so I asked Henry to buy it for me. I combed in a generous amount after I took a shower and let it dry until my hair felt like the end of a broom. Then I combed it out so it would have some body and be straight. Except for the waves at the end.

My hair grew slowly, and I had to get it cut short each summer before I showed up for my job as a seasonal ranger, so at the end of the school year it was barely long enough to form a vestigial ponytail. My father seemed wryly amused, but my mother was aghast. "My God, you look awful," she said, and she was right. I have a photograph taken on the day Kath graduated from UC Santa Cruz. She's standing between me and her boyfriend, Gerhard, who had shoulder-length hair of the sort I fantasized for myself. By contrast, I look like a cross between Gene Wilder and Don King.

My high forehead began to climb higher in my early twenties, so I started combing my hair at an angle toward the front. It flew back when I walked into a wind, and I would reflexively reach up and rake it forward, again and again, as if I could will it into place. The first time I heard *Look, he's going bald!* I realized I wasn't fooling anyone, but I wasn't ready to acknowledge that I'd moved beyond *receding hairline.* I continued to rake and smooth and pat until I concluded that a bare scalp, even a pale one like mine, was better than a Zero Mostel comb-over. I asked my barber to cut my hair shorter. I bought a hair dryer so I could overwhelm most of the waviness. When nothing was left in front except a small, downy patch, I shaved it each morning along with my cheeks and chin.

Going bald in my 30s meant that I didn't have to confront the evidence of my mortality all at once. By the time I began to despair at the bags under my eyes and the thickening at my waist, my hair had been gone for a decade. Had I been a George Clooney lookalike and thinning hair my only flaw, I might have paid good money to plant new hair where old hair had thrown in the towel. But I knew that even with a full head of hair I would win no prizes, and I hadn't forgotten how much I'd disliked my hair when I still had some.

A full head of hair is a sexual bargaining chip like firm breasts. We say these things don't matter, but we know they do. We know that, for the most part, the hunks pair up with the total babes and the rest of us take what's left, even though we desire beauty just as much.

When we're at parties, we don't poke a man's beer belly or tug on a woman's sagging breasts, but for some reason it's OK to tease bald men about their baldness. I try to pre-empt the tired jokes and deliver the punch lines myself. Yep, I save a lot of money on shampoo.

I wear a Giants cap when I'm out running errands. It's more convenient than smearing sunscreen on my head, and it makes me feel less old. More to the point, it means that the people I pass on the street, if they notice me at all, can only wonder whether or not I have hair, and that's a small comfort.

Daphne Hits the Books

"Homework!? No!" The neighbors hear
A now familiar cry.
Does Daphne have a paper due?
The neighbors nod and sigh.

Does Daphne do her homework
Right away as she's been taught?
Is Daphne done by dinnertime?
Why no, in fact, she's not.

Daphne dips potato chips.
She calls her friend Babette.
She tootle-oos, she changes shoes
(She hasn't started yet).

She hears a beat and taps her feet.
She hums a favorite tune.
She draws a rose, explores her nose
(She'll start her paper soon).

She counts the ceiling tiles a while
And hugs her teddy, Eddie.

She rearranges pocket change
(She's close to being ready).

She shuns advice, she sneezes twice,
She thinks she may be ill.
She takes a timely cookie break
(Procrastination, still).

She sits and stares, she sulks and glares,
She feels as if she's mired.
She wonders why, she swats a fly
(Just wait, she'll get inspired).

When Daphne does her homework
It's a struggle harsh and cruel.
(Simon, as you might suspect,
Completed his at school.)

TOY STORIES III:
I STILL HAVE MINE

TEN CENTS. THAT WAS MY ALLOWANCE WHEN I WAS NINE, and I spent it the same way each week. I turned east off Waters Avenue on my way home from Emerson Elementary School, walked down the hill to Red Wing Market and bought two packs of 1958 Topps baseball cards. I did this three or four years before I first swung a bat or listened to a baseball game on the radio. I bought the cards because I'd seen my classmates shuffling through stacks of them and I liked the bright colors on the fronts and the pen and ink caricatures of the players on the backs.

Each card was flawless when I unfolded the waxed paper wrapping—sharp-cornered, slightly convex from top to bottom, and gently perfumed by the accompanying stick of stale bubble gum.

The cards for Vic Power and Rocky Bridges were among the first I acquired. Looking at them now, I see that neither Vic nor Rocky wore batting gloves, that both were right-handed and that Bridges choked up on his bat. But what I saw then was that Bridges had something—a walnut, maybe—stuffed into one of his cheeks, and that Power was a Negro. There were a few Japanese kids in my class—I gave my best valentine to

Karen Tsukiji one year—but everyone else at my school and in our neighborhood was white. When we drove past Seattle's colored neighborhood on Capitol Hill, my father might have pointed it out as he would the University District or Green Lake, but without suggesting that it was anything other than a distinct part of town. I regarded the Negro ballplayers on my cards in somewhat the same way, noticing the different shades of brown on their faces just as I noticed the fresh yellows and corals of my mother's snapdragons.

Had I first seen baseball cards in 1956 or 1957, I would have spent my allowance on something else. But the Topps cards in 1958 were bright and cheery. Each player's headshot had been carefully trimmed out and placed on a background of pure color. Yellow, red and blue were the most common, but I preferred the New York Yankees cards, which were shades of a burnt orange that fit right in with baseball gloves. (I didn't have a Mickey Mantle, but I did have a Tony Kubek, a Don Larsen and, yes, a Marv Throneberry.) Green was good, too. The Milwaukee Braves had green cards—a rich, leafy green for Warren Spahn, a lighter green for Eddie Mathews, lime sherbet for Del Rice. The Detroit Tigers cards were Pepto Bismol pink, an odd choice, I thought, but a distinct one.

They were called trading cards, but I didn't trade them. Or draw beards on the players' faces or clothespin a card between the spokes on my bicycle wheels to make flappy engine noises. I studied my cards. I set them out on the floor and sorted them by team. Then I sorted them by color. I looked for my favorite nicknames, like Whammy and Moose, and for odd names like Johnny Kucks and Elvis Tappe. I staged contests for the goofiest looking player until I realized that Cleveland's Don Mossi would always win because he had the biggest Dumbo ears.

Before I gathered up the cards and put them back in their box, I would look one more time at the mysterious Missing Bat Players. Elston Howard was one of them, apparently swinging in such a way that his bat was entirely concealed by his arms. But someone must have done an airbrush job on Gino Cimoli, and Red Wilson is missing not just his bat, but all of his left arm and most of his right. Old war wounds?

I bought a few packs of baseball cards in 1959, but they were too modern looking and they didn't have as much color. Two of the players even posed without their caps. Because I encased them in clear plastic sleeves and didn't handle them much, the '59 cards have aged gracefully. The cards for average players like Steve Bilko aren't worth all that much, even in mint condition, but my Sandy Koufax, it turns out, is worth somewhere between $600 and $4,000. At least that's what it says online.

A BERKELEY TRILOGY: 1967-1971

TEAR GAS

Technically it was a powder. The Tactical Squadron of the Alameda County Sheriff's Office—the feared Blue Meanies—tried to break up crowds of demonstrators by dispensing it from hurled canisters that looked like a cross between a hand grenade and a can of your uncle's shaving cream. Compressed gas at the core dispersed the powder that was packed around it. Voila, crowd control. Or at least crowd relocation.

One afternoon, Henry came home from a demonstration with an empty tear gas canister he intended to convert into a political work of art. Demonstrators were supposed to throw the canisters back at the cops, but Henry claimed he hadn't found it until after things simmered down. He thumped it against the curb to knock loose the last of the powder before he brought it into the house, but even so we all sneezed for a week while he painted it red, white and blue, and entombed it in a clear Plexiglas cube.

I don't know what it was about red, white and blue and cubes, but somewhere around the same time, I built a wood framework for a cube three feet on a side and swathed it in white canvas. I asked Henry to take a photograph of me standing behind a chain link fence. I enlarged the photo to the size of the cube, made a pattern from it and then painted the image on the cube. In red, white and blue. Did I believe that I'd been imprisoned in some way by my own government? No, not especially. But had my perspective been influenced by all the Leftists and Marxists and Black Radicals who were squabbling about whose revolution would go down first? Um, yes.

Well before I enrolled at UC Berkeley, my nascent political beliefs had begun to drift to the left. I'd been on the campus twice with Arcata High's delegation to the Model United Nations—we represented Malaysia and then Mali—and although what impressed me most at the time was the Lotus Europa I saw zipping down Bancroft Way, my classmates and I had also been across the bay to San Francisco. We attended a performance by The Committee. We bought peace buttons in four colors at The Print Mint, flipped through copies of Alan Ginsberg's *Howl* at City Lights bookstore, and drove through the Haight-Ashbury. When a fellow student got suspended for refusing to cut his hair so that it didn't touch his ears, I circulated a petition asking the Arcata High School Board to loosen up the dress code.

Within a week after I began my freshman year at UC Berkeley, I'd been to a recruitment meeting for SDS, but I didn't join. I did stay up all night to take part in a Stop The Draft Week march to the Oakland Induction Center, keeping well back of the front lines to avoid being clubbed, and returning to my dorm room exhausted and depressed.

Soon enough, I'd be able to see all the action I wanted without leaving Berkeley. Protests against the Vietnam War? The Third World Strike? ROTC on campus? The cause varied, but whatever it was, it was often the subject of a noon rally featuring an angry speaker standing on the steps of Sproul Hall, shouting into a bullhorn and jabbing a finger at the assembled crowd. Usually his (or occasionally her) indignant rant trailed off and the crowd dwindled and everyone went to their afternoon classes. But at other times, in response to a news story about the bombing of Hanoi, or to violent arrests at a demonstration at another university, the rhetoric and the call-and-response chanting would build to a critical mass and the crowd would head off on another righteous march across campus or down nearby Telegraph Avenue.

The banks on Telegraph—including the Bank of America branch, where I had my first checking account—were easy targets for the proto-anarchists who invited themselves to these marches. One thrown rock could shatter a plate glass window, and that made it official.

Bottles were smashed against walls. Fists pounded the hoods of cars. The cacophony was exhilarating: the tromping of hundreds of pairs of feet, the cheering and chanting and Indian war whoops, the crashes and thuds.

The merchants on Telegraph Avenue—aka the Bloodsucking Capitalists—soon learned to keep a few sheets of plywood on hand. The banks eventually bricked up most of their windows even as the marches moved west to downtown Berkeley. It was a longer walk from campus, but the police needed more manpower to cordon off the wider streets, and the construction materials for the BART tunnel along Shattuck Avenue were an abundant source of throwable objects. One afternoon, I walked down Shattuck five minutes after a particularly violent mob had passed through. They'd broken windows at several car dealerships and speared 2x4s through the windshields of the floor models. The owner of a nearby jewelry store was standing in his doorway holding a pistol.

If the action was still going when rush hour began, the streets would quickly become gridlocked, and demonstrators could play cat and mouse with the police among the stopped cars, but this was unusual because most of us wanted to get home in time to watch the day's mayhem on the evening news. I knew there were true believers who were justifiably angry about the

Vietnam War, and I saw people pleading to keep the marches nonviolent, but for some the lawlessness was irresistible. I was amazed that blatant criminal acts could be committed in broad daylight, one after another, with little likelihood that anyone would be held accountable. And my roommates were just the sort of bad influence my father feared. Henry tried to fire bomb an old shingle-clad building that housed the politically incorrect Center for Asian Studies, and I'd seen Junior throw a rock at a helicopter flying so low that the rock arced over the fuselage and broke a window in the Life Sciences Building.

I read the pigs-did-this-pigs-did-that *Berkeley Barb* and rarely left town, so it didn't occur to me to wonder whether blue collar workers in Concord or San Leandro saw things the way I did. And it wasn't as if I'd come to the University anxious to prepare for my life's work. I'd come because it was inconceivable to my father that I wouldn't go straight on to college, and inconceivable to me that I wouldn't do what he expected. More to the point, my student deferment would keep me out of Vietnam. I was treading water, but the lax academic standards of the day allowed me to maintain a B average and still head for the streets whenever things got interesting.

I was cautious. I never threw anything, never set

anything on fire, always stayed at the edge of the action and always moved when the cops said move. But I was there. There outside the perimeter when the cops sealed off Sproul Plaza and a helicopter dropped CS gas on the demonstrators. There when the Blue Meanies cordoned off an entire city block, arrested five hundred people, and shipped them off to the county jail for the night. I was mesmerized by the violence and fascinated by the surreal pageantry—the squadrons of Berkeley police with color-coded armbands, and the CHP cruisers, four patrolmen to a car, commuting to the campus each morning to assemble in the parking lot below the tennis courts on College Avenue in readiness for a likely afternoon riot.

In the end, everyone got more or less what they wanted. The television stations got great footage, the demonstrators got plenty of exposure, the cops got to fire tear gas and crack a few heads, and people got arrested, but the charges were often reduced or dropped, and no one got seriously hurt. No one, that is, until People's Park.

I'd been up most of the night grinding away on an architecture project, so I was still asleep when Will burst into our apartment at midday. "Quick! Get dressed! You won't believe the shit that's going down out there!" He had a red bandanna tied around his head. He was flushed, breathing hard, anxious to dash back out and rejoin Junior and Henry. We agreed that I would try to rendezvous with the three of them in ten minutes, and he was out the door. I could hear whoops and pops and squealing tires off toward Telegraph Avenue. A familiar roiling began in my gut as I hurried into my clothes. I hadn't missed everything, had I?

I was angry about Vietnam and vaguely sympathetic to the grievances of the Black Panthers and Chicano activists, but I didn't find it particularly outrageous that the University planned to build student housing on a piece of property it owned in South Campus. The existing buildings had been demolished, and the empty lot had evolved into a sort of hippie encampment with flutes and drums, bins of free clothing, nightly bonfires and couples balling in sleeping bags. The lot soon had a name: People's Park. Friends who'd been there in the evenings said it was a mellow scene, but the University couldn't have been pleased with the lack of sanitation and the drugs and the occasional scuffles. Late one night, they evicted everyone and put up a fence, which The People tore down the next day. The University put the fence back up and drew a line in the dirt. The People crossed the line. Things got ugly.

I didn't know as I ran down to Telegraph that James Rector had been shot and killed on a rooftop overlooking the street, or that other demonstrators had been shot and injured. But it was clear that both sides had upped the ante. Black smoke curled from an overturned police car in the middle of an intersection. I saw a man with a camera—a plainclothes cop?—being slugged and kicked. If the protest had begun as an organized march, it had long since fragmented into small bands of rioters darting through the streets all over South Campus. I didn't see my roommates until we grouped around the television that evening, flipping from channel to channel.

Governor Reagan called in the National Guard. Soldiers with rifles soon occupied People's Park in force, and they set up a broad perimeter around campus. I passed through one of their checkpoints on my way to and from class. In a way, I was relieved to see them. Only the truly deranged would now instigate the sort of violence that could provoke live bullets, and, unlike the Blue Meanies, some of whom were said to be Vietnam vets with short fuses, these guys had become Guardsmen to stay out of the war. They weren't itching to crack our ribs. Some of them chatted quietly with students who lived on the streets where they stood guard, and some of the students brought them food.

Junior, not surprisingly, had a different take on things, and he was pissed. One evening, as he and Will and I crouched on the roof of our apartment building watching the Blue Meanies cruise our street in their squad cars, he picked up an egg-sized decorative rock from the roof. Will and I looked at him nervously. *You've got to be kidding, Junior.* But he wasn't. He threw the rock at the next squad car that passed beneath us and nailed the deputy in the passenger-side seat on the forearm. We were back in our apartment with textbooks in our laps by the time they knocked on the door. I suppose they could have lined us up to look for tar on the bottoms of our shoes. I suppose they could have done a lot of things—they already had. But we were lucky.

In 1965, less than four years earlier, I'd attended a summer school sponsored by the Junior Statesmen of America. Twenty-five of us studied political science for a month at a private high school surrounded by Central Valley orchards. There was one black kid among us, a sweet guy. We formed an unofficial chapter of the Ku Klux Klan and elected him president. I remember how shy he was, how anguished by his crush on one of the girls. I recognized his name a few years later when he made the evening news. He'd tried to set off a bomb at San Francisco State, and it exploded prematurely and blinded him. If I'd been a little closer to the front lines, if

I'd waited a little longer before I turned and ran from the cops, if I'd been on Telegraph Avenue when James Rector was shot, what might have happened to me?

ALL NIGHTERS

The worst part was walking at dawn from the architecture building back to our apartment in a scratchy eyed, sleep deprived haze. These were the only times I was up early enough to notice the quiet streets and soft colors and the cooing of the doves. They made me sad.

The architecture building was Wurster Hall. It had been built in the '60s as the replacement for a brown shingle firetrap on the other side of campus, and there was no confusing the two. Wurster was a workmanlike tip of the hat to postwar European Brutalism. Lots of raw concrete and textured plywood—the correctional facility aesthetic with splinters. There were offices and classrooms on the lower levels, but we students spent most of our time at our drafting tables in the design studios in the north tower. We had three core courses each quarter—ordinary classes with reasonable amounts of homework—and one design class that periodically kept most of us up all night. We scorned the married guys with crew cuts who worked at home and showed up well rested for their critiques during finals week.

The studio floors were completely open except for a couple conference rooms, but each drafting table had a partition attached to the back of it, and by grouping the tables in particular ways (and looting extra partitions from other floors) we could assemble enclosures that recalled our fort-building years. Any student with a truck and a comfort level with larceny could make a late night trip downtown to rip off shoring timbers from the BART construction site. The timbers were assembled into sturdy platforms a foot or two above the bare concrete floor, and some of the desks were perched on them as if they were little islands. We brought in hot plates and a stereo system and rigged a few bed sheets to serve as canopies to soften the fluorescent lighting.

I had taken drafting classes in high school, but I hadn't learned how to set up the vanishing points for a perspective drawing and I couldn't draw freehand, so I built scale models of all my design projects. For one class it was collapsible displays for street vendors on Union Square, for the next it was low-cost student housing above the BART right of way. The most elaborate model I built was for a whaling station. Decades before, there had actually been one in nearby Richmond, and I designed its replacement. I concluded that a unistrut grid cocked at forty five degrees was the right way to avoid mid-span columns that would impede movement of the carcasses (this was before *Songs of the Humpback Whale*). I built the model from thousands of pieces of balsa wood the size of kitchen matches. This entailed much work in the wee hours.

Many architecture students drank coffee to stay awake during the long nights, and some of them did speed, but I didn't like the taste of coffee and thought drugs were for entertainment, so I drank Coke and smoked cigarettes and ate cookies from the vending machines downstairs. I got jittery from all the sugar and caffeine. My feet swelled from sitting too long and my body ached as if I had the flu.

The stereo played without surcease—Cream and Santana and The Moody Blues, hour after hour. Otis Redding sat on the dock of a bay so often he wore a hole in the seat of his pants. He sounded woeful, like he wasn't getting enough sleep either. When the eastern horizon began to glow, someone would cue up "Here Comes the Sun." It was a cruel moment.

One night without sleep wouldn't ruin me, but two in a row were an ordeal. My mood sank, my efficiency sank with it, and I expended as much effort trying to stay motivated and focused as I did measuring and cutting and gluing. When I finished whatever I was doing and went home, I was so wired it took an hour to fall asleep, and it was contorted sleep when it came. I woke up feeling nearly as wasted as I'd been before I went to bed.

The conclusion to some of these exhausting marathons was an end-of-the-quarter critique of our work. We took our projects into a conference room where our professor had used wine to bribe several colleagues into serving as jurors. These jurors used our projects as target practice as they espoused their conflicting theories of Design and Social Responsibility, zinging each other with snide comments in the best academic tradition, particularly after they'd finished off the wine. I listened to one such skirmish while my project was being critiqued. I was leaning against the wall next to it, eating an ice cream sandwich. I fell asleep.

UNFIT FOR MILITARY SERVICE

My four years as an undergraduate were bracketed by two trips to the Oakland Induction Center, the first to try to keep other young men from being sent to Vietnam, and the second to do the same for myself.

I had no idea what or where Vietnam was until I was in high school in the mid '60s. When the name began to stick in my consciousness, I assumed without reflection that America was right to shore up a nation imperiled by Communism. It wasn't until my junior year that I noticed that most of the raffish classmates I quietly admired were against the war, and the drive-at-the-limit citizens who jeered at their peace buttons mostly supported it.

During my senior year, I wrote a term paper about the Vietnam War in Mr. Storm's Problems of American Democracy class. I did my research by reading back issues of *Ramparts* magazine. I reiterated the basic points, that the division between North and South was supposed to have been an interim partition after the French left, that Ho Chi Minh enjoyed popular support throughout the country, and so forth. It was a typical adolescent tirade, and Mr. Storm gave me an A without comment.

I spent little time thinking about how the Vietnam War might affect me personally until I was in college and my birthday came up 48th in the Selective Service System's first draft lottery. Then—because any number below 200 was bad news—I thought about it a lot. I'd heard that skinny guys like me sometimes served as tunnel rats, the first soldiers to crawl in on elbows and knees—flashlight in one hand, pistol in the other—to look for enemy soldiers. My first plan to avoid such a fate was to apply for Conscientious Objector status. My cousin Don, a longtime pacifist, had served as a CO several years before, performing his alternative service as an orderly at a mental hospital. Don and I talked, and he probed gently at the reasoning behind my contention that I would fight for a just cause, say, Israel. I wrote a first draft of my application, but it was one of the few such things I didn't keep, and I've long forgotten what line of argument I set out or why I didn't pursue CO status further. Instead, I looked into joining the Coast Guard, and applied for admission to graduate school at Canada's McGill University so I'd be out of the country when my student deferment expired, but these were narrow, crowded paths.

Motivated more by fear than principle, I knew I would refuse induction—and maybe be sent to prison—before I would go to Vietnam. I enrolled in a How to Avoid the Draft class at a Catholic church a few blocks from campus. It was a surprisingly well-ordered and thorough curriculum addressing all aspects of the Selective Service System: how it was organized, how it functioned, how to exploit its ambiguities and hamper its processes with diversions and appeals. I took careful notes, especially about the various disabilities and ailments that might get me classified 4F—physically unfit to serve.

There were three possibilities. The first, conceivably,

was eczema. One of my earliest memories is of the soothing effect of the cloth strips my mother soaked in warm Epsom salts and wrapped around my inflamed forearms. The condition cleared during my childhood, but the crooks of my elbows were red and cracked for most of my adolescence. Now, perhaps, there would be a payoff for my discomfort. I wrote to our family doctor requesting a letter describing the condition.

My lower back was a more likely cause for disqualification. I'd fallen hard during a basketball game in a high school PE class and aggravated the injury while working as a janitor's assistant the following summer. I spent two days in bed with sizzling jolts of pain coursing down the sciatic nerve in my left leg. A specialist said I had an unpronounceable six-syllable deformity in my lumbar vertebrae—cartilage where I should have had bone. The deformity, if severe enough, was a way out. I again wrote requesting a letter.

Finally, I learned that it was possible to be so thin that I'd be unfit to serve, even as a tunnel rat. I weighed 127 pounds. If I lost nine of them, I'd slip below the minimum permissible weight for my height, and buy ninety days before they could weigh me again. So, a week before my pre-induction physical, I began my idea of a suitable crash diet, eating only round steak, hard boiled eggs and raw carrots, and drinking only grapefruit juice and water. I didn't have a scale, but by the day of my physical, my ribs were nicely defined. I walked the five miles to the Induction Center in downtown Oakland. I had no idea how the buses ran, and I thought I might lose another ounce or two on the way.

The physical was just as it had been portrayed in the movie *Alice's Restaurant*. There were dozens and dozens of young men in white jockey shorts. Bright, freshly laundered shorts, or grayed shorts worn through and unraveling. Our physiques were all over the map. An orderly walked past with a tray of blood samples, and the fattest guy near me immediately paled and dropped to the floor.

We moved in groups from station to station. We stood balancing on one foot and then the other. We breathed deeply and coughed. We lowered our shorts and bent over in ragged unison. We arrived at the catch-all station where college boys like me handed over letters from our doctors. There were a lot of us with letters by 1971.

"Let's see what you've got," said the military doctor, a black gentleman sitting across from me at his desk. I gave him the letter about my eczema and he glanced at it. "What about now?" he asked. "Do you have any now?" I showed him a pink patch on my forearm the size of a nickel. I'd worn sweaters for weeks to encourage it. He chuckled. "Anything else?" I showed him the letter about my back. He looked at the paperwork documenting my height and weight, and noted the odd effect my diet had had on the albumen level in my blood. He furrowed his brow and asked me, in a voice as neutral as he could manage, "Would you like to join the Armed Forces?"

"No, sir."

"Are you sure? You could see some interesting parts of the world."

"Yes, sir. I'm sure."

"You can save all your pay while you're in, you know. You'd have a lot of money when you got out."

"I'm sure. Sir." He looked at me as if disappointed and sighed a theatrical sigh.

"Alright, then." *Thunk*. He stamped my papers *4F: Unfit for Military Service* and handed them back to me.

Though faint from hunger, I walked the five miles back to Berkeley. I stopped at Lucca's Delicatessen in North Oakland to buy a box of fresh raviolis, a pint of meat sauce and some sliced provolone. I called my parents to tell them I'd flunked my physical. I ate dinner alone.

The Alphabet

A is for Alice, who's taking a snooze.
B is for Barney, who butters his shoes.

C is for Clara, who strolls into town.
D is for Devon, who strolls upside down.

E is for Ellen, who gargles her peas.
F is for Franco, who lives overseas.

G is for Greta, who hitches her britches.
H is for Henry, who keeps her in stitches.

I is for Ida inside a giraffe.
J is for Jordan, who tries not to laugh.

K is for Katie, who juggles cabooses.
L is for Leonard, who dances with mooses.

M is for Molly, who tickles her aunt.
N is for Norton, who'd like to but can't.

O's for Olivia, down in the dumps.
P is for Perry, who loaned her the mumps.

Q is for… who has a name with a Q?
R is for Roscoe. He hasn't a clue.

S is for Sarah who squeaks when she sneezes.
Tea is for Trevor whenever he pleases.

U is for Uma, from Yuma no doubt.
V is for Vinnie. He's checking it out.

W's Wanda or Wilma or Wendy.
X is for Xerxes: historic, yet trendy.

Y's for Yolanda. What else could we do?
Z is for Zeppo. Thank goodness we're through!

Sat the little Hiawatha

Judy, Kath, my parents and Camera Shy

I requested blue frosting

Two birds with one stone

The Bayside Grasshoppers

Eleventh grade

Kath graduates from UC Santa
Cruz with her boyfriend and her
shaggy brother

My parents at Judy's wedding
in Hawaii

The biggest mushroom
she ever found

Looking for jade

934 Fickle Hill Road
under construction

Don't say we didn't
warn you

Finishing the cabin at
Pear Point

His characteristic stance

Opening night at the SF Opera
with Claire

The photo I used for
my personal ad

Marie Santucci,
Emotional Dismantler

Basic mountaineering in
Jordache jeans

Bonding with a yak en route
to Everest Base Camp

Rapids on the Natla-Keele

Alexandra Fiord,
Ellesmere Island

Jumping over a glacial meltwater stream,
Ellesmere Island

My first previously owned Porsche

Faux Pas feigning innocence

Above the Mountain River in Canada's Northwest Territories

Light Cancellation Marks

Like all kids who collect stamps, I started at the age of nine. We had just moved to California and Judy had gone off to college and somehow in all the packing and unpacking I came across her stamp collection and decided to keep it. Or maybe she gave it to me. Either way, it was a beginner's album about as thick as a *Reader's Digest*, with one page per country, except that important countries like England and France got two or three pages. Conversely, some pages were divvied up between several small countries I'd never heard of. All the pages were divided into grids that could accommodate stamps of different sizes and shapes, and some of the rectangles framed black-and-white facsimiles of the stamps that were supposed to rest on top of them. Drawn to orderliness as always, I found it quite satisfying to lick a pale green Dennison's stamp hinge, stick it to the back of, say, a British five pence stamp with a left facing profile of Queen Elizabeth, and superimpose the stamp on its likeness just as the album's publisher intended.

Based on the few stamps scattered through her album, Judy would have known little of this satisfaction. Her stamps looked forlorn in their isolation, so I set about finding them some companions. I had a couple hundred foreign coins stored in a jar, mostly leftover pocket change that various adults had given me after they returned from abroad. It seemed to me that these coins could be fairly exchanged for stamps based more or less on weight, say fifty stamps for one of those Chinese coins with a square hole in the middle. So, during recess at College Elementary School, I dickered with trading partners who were amenable to this line of reasoning, and acquired hundreds of stamps before I ran out of tradable currency.

In the meantime, my mother mentioned my nascent hobby to her friend, Hortense, with whom she occasionally hunted wild mushrooms. Hortense was a retired biology professor who had the local mycology down cold, so there was little danger that she or my mother would mistakenly sauté a panful of Death Angels and wipe out an entire dinner party. I liked Hortense. She didn't make the usual distinction between adults and children, and she was strikingly eccentric. She lived out on the bottomlands west of Arcata in a faux half-timbered Tudor house where grumpy cats ruled the kitchen counters. She was a meticulous artist, and she had painted a full size human skeleton—wearing cowboy boots, holstered six guns, a Stetson and a red neckerchief—on the inside of the door to her basement.

My mother said Hortense had an unusual sense of humor.

Hortense's son had also collected stamps in his youth, and when she heard that I'd taken up the hobby, she gave me a cardboard box containing his Five Star General stamp album, a 1951 edition of the Scott stamp catalog, and an assortment of smaller boxes and glassine envelopes filled with stamps, thousands of them. I was gobsmacked. Could this be divine compensation for the cherished Tinkertoys my parents had given away when we moved to California?

I systematically examined my windfall and soon became more an organizer than a collector. I spent quiet afternoons sorting loose stamps by country and then by chronological order and denomination. I arrayed them in little please-don't-sneeze piles on the living room floor and compared them to the stamps already mounted in my new album, which had five times the capacity of Judy's and a fair number of pages that were nearly full. I found an occasional gap I could fill, but mostly I rested easy knowing that all the Czechoslovakian 30 haleru, for example, were together at last.

I found that the nations of the world were not equally represented. For every stamp from Republique du Togo or Republica Oriental del Uruguay, there were dozens from each Western European country and a hundred from the United States. Not only that, but the more obscure the country, the less likely it was that the stamps had actually been licked, stuck to an envelope, mailed, canceled and delivered. The Five Star General had three stamps each from dozens of exotic backwaters like Guadeloupe, The British Solomon Islands and Upper Volta, and all were flawless specimens touched only by tweezers. Had it ever been possible to mail a letter from Basutoland to Niue, or were the stamps from these alleged countries printed and sold solely for the entertainment of philatelists?

The Five Star General allotted almost three pages to the stamps of Finland, and here at least I was able to make a significant contribution to the work of my predecessor. My mother was a Finnish native, and co-respondence had been exchanged for decades between the old country and the new. I had so many different Finnish stamps that I wallpapered FINLAND, overran FIUME (an independent city annexed to Italy in 1924) and would have invaded FRANCE if the album hadn't been bound with Chicago screws so I could take it apart to add new pages.

Stamp collecting was my first direct introduction to global diversity. I discovered that not everyone on the planet speaks English, that to those who live there

Austria is Österreich, Italy is Italia and Spain is España. I discovered that the Roman alphabet is not universal. It could be found on all the stamps of Europe, so that Danmark, Nederland and Belgique were easily recognizable. It was also used in Helvetia, Magyarorszag and Shqiptare, which, if my album was correct, were Switzerland, Hungary and Albania. But as you moved farther south and east, things got complicated. There were both Roman letters and Greek letters on Greek stamps, but neither spelled *Greece*. Bulgarian stamps had Cyrillic characters. I knew that some of the letters of the Cyrillic alphabet did not represent the same sounds as their Roman counterparts, but I still looked at Bulgaria in Cyrillic and saw Bubbawrapner.

Growing up within historical spitting distance of the Second World War, my grade school friends and I had a dark, persistent fascination with Hitler and the German military. The black letter *Deutsches Reich* on most prewar German stamps was as sinister to us as the swastika. Some of the German stamps from the '30s featured heroic Aryan soil tillers and sledge hammerers, but many displayed the denomination only: 100 marks, 1,000 marks, then fifty thousand, a million, a hundred million, ten billion. The hyperinflation that, in part, brought Hitler to power was depicted right there on page 99, and then, on page 101, was der Führer's pinched and sallow profile in a dozen denominations and colors.

Like most collectors, I wondered what my collection was worth, and I paged through the Scott catalog to look up the oldest of the stamps I'd inherited. A cancelled 15 cent denomination of the United States Colombian Exposition Issue of 1893, for example, listed at $85.00 for a specimen in *fine condition*. I was amazed to think that anyone would pay that much money for a perforated piece of paper the size of the Tumble Dry tag on my Fruit of the Looms. But my specimen didn't have particularly good color, it wasn't centered, and the cancellation mark was so heavy it practically obliterated a third of the stamp. I had lots of more recent stamps that were in *fine condition*, and nearly all of them were worth seventeen cents. Assuming anyone wanted to buy them.

It was apparent, reading here and there in the catalog, that stamp collecting could be tedious, at least from where I sat. Many of the older United States stamps had been printed in several versions so similar you needed a magnifying glass to tell them apart. Subtle differences in color were also important, and there was much ado about watermarks. Serious collectors moved on from single stamps to first day covers and plate blocks. I found none of this intriguing. I liked stamps because they were colorful, because they often had attractive images on them and because they were historic artifacts. Abyssinia had vanished, but its stamps still existed.

Once I'd imposed order on the loose stamps Hortense had given me, I began to lose interest. I steamed contemporary stamps off of envelopes for a while, and sent away for *A Thousand Foreign Stamps for a Dollar*, but the idea of active collecting didn't take. I would have been more inclined to dump out all the loose stamps, mix them up and start over. But when I buy stamps at the post office, I always ask to see the commemoratives. And when I pay my bills each month, I stick the stamp down square to the envelope and about an eighth of an inch in from the top and right edges, though I don't imagine anyone else notices.

We'll Make a List

We'll make a list of everything
That is or ever was.
We'll start with Abyssinia
And stop for lunch because

A proper list will take some time
Or else we may forget
A perfect day in April
Or a tenor clarinet

Let's see. There are...

Viking ships and chocolate chips
And elevator shoes
And tambourines and time machines
And tantalizing clues

And applesauce and dental floss
And disappearing ink
And barber shops and halter tops
In seven shades of pink

And fairy tales and great blue whales
Who seldom stop to chat

And Mongol hordes and harpsichords
And Mister Murphy's cat

And kings and queens and navy beans
And stacks of buttered toast
And rubber ducks and pickup trucks
That drive from coast to coast

And ladybugs and shaving mugs
And fuzzy grey cocoons
And polar bears in rocking chairs
On lazy afternoons

And Buddhist monks in swimming trunks
And crystal chandeliers
And double doors and dinosaurs
And tenants in arrears

And double dates and shipping crates
And Crazy Eights and figure skates
And weekly rates and license plates
And Incas from Peru

And double chins and muffin tins
And violins and bowling pins
And frozen Finns and loony bins
And pumpernickel, too

And mothers' smiles and crocodiles
And Mister Ed and Charo
We've covered lots of ground today…
We'll finish up tomorrow.

NOTES

BACK WHEN THE TICKET PRICES WERE MORE REASONABLE, I attended San Francisco Symphony concerts on a regular basis. My seats (I had two, one for me and one for a guest) were directly to the left of the orchestra. They were vulnerable to an overdose of brass and percussion, but I didn't mind because I could see the conductor's facial expressions and his enraptured sighs, and I could link each sound to the instruments that produced it. I often thought there could be no profession more satisfying than the creation of music. Who else but musicians get a standing ovation at the end of each workday?

During my earliest years, our family had one of those plump freestanding radio consoles with a record player you could slide out to play old 78s. My father had a dozen or so classical albums to go with it, but they were so cumbersome that I looked at the illustrations on the covers more often than I heard them played. I was drawn to the gaudy landscape depicted on the cover of *The Grand Canyon Suite*, a dramatic foreground in deep reds and browns framing a horseman at the base of yellow cliffs. I studied it as though such a place might exist. I liked the *Suite's* clip-clopping and braying before I was old enough to differentiate between donkeys and musicians, or to know that an orchestra had to record the music before we could listen to it in our living room.

My mother listened to the radio as she ironed my father's shirts and tended our old tub of a washing machine. I recall snippets—Arthur Godfrey and his ukulele; newsmen talking about people named Eisenhower and McCarthy; "This Old House"—but I preferred KXA, the classical station my father was more likely to tune in to when he was home. Classical music was soothing to a child easily frightened.

When I was six, my father informed me that I was about to begin taking piano lessons. Not surprisingly, I didn't want to, because I was wary of anything new and because I didn't want to make mistakes and be corrected. And why did he want me to play the piano anyway? I'd shown no interest in musical instruments. More to the point, we didn't have a piano, so I was supposed to practice my scales and "See Saw Ride" and "Daffodil Serenade" on a paper keyboard until we got one. I took the bogus keyboard into my parents' bedroom and stared at it for fifteen minutes each afternoon. Years later I found out that my father had wanted to take piano lessons when he was young, but wasn't able to.

Things improved a bit when a well-worn upright piano arrived at our house and I could play real notes. I liked my piano teacher. Her name was Catholine Chihara, and her brother, Ted, was one of my father's colleagues in the mathematics department at Seattle University. Catholine was Japanese American, and though her family had been interned during the Second World War, her parents now owned a successful appliance store in Seattle, and her brothers, Charlie and Paul, would become, respectively, a professor of philosophy and a composer. I admired the Chiharas and enjoyed visiting their home. It looked like any other house from the street, but inside there were many richly colored objects of silk and lacquered wood.

Catholine's parents hosted a recital by all of her students, including Kath and me. I would play two pieces. The first one was called "Rose Petals," and the sheet music for the second one had a shiny copper cover with Siamese dancers. It was in a minor key. I rehearsed these simple pieces for hours because I hoped practice would make me less nervous. The recital took place on a pleasant Sunday afternoon. My performance may not have been lyrical, but it was accurate, and I took as little of the audience's time as possible. Kath also played without incident, but a student named Paul lost his place and his composure and sat crying at the piano. That was why I had practiced so hard, to avoid making a mistake in front of all those people. But Paul recovered, and after cake and ice cream, he and Kath and I posed with the other students for a group photo in front of the Chihara's house. I was wearing a red bow tie, a sports jacket and the first of several pairs of wool slacks that would itch me without mercy every time I had to dress up.

During our first year in Arcata, I think we attended nearly every public event Humboldt State College had to offer. My father may have wanted to suggest to the college community that we were pleased to become a part of it, but I'd also just turned nine and Kath would soon be eight and my father probably felt we were old enough to appreciate a variety of new experiences. So we attended all the football games (the Lumberjacks were a great team in those days) and a couple basketball games while we were at it. We also went to see kid-friendly plays like *Outward Bound* and *Waiting for Godot*.

And then there were the chamber music concerts, which made my wool-clad thighs itch with ferocity. A string quartet of music department professors performed on occasional Sunday evenings in a classroom. Members of the small audiences fingered their mimeographed programs and waited to applaud at the end of each piece. One of the violinists rocked back and forth and turned red while he played. I found this amusing—I imagined he was sitting on the toilet—but to my ears the music was as dry as peanut butter stuck to the roof of my mouth. My father usually fell asleep before the first piece had run its course, but we would go to the next concert anyway. Once, a black music major played a solo on the trombone. Kath and I had never seen an embouchure up close before, and we were only partially successful at keeping our faces straight. Our father was quietly furious because he assumed that his peers would see our behavior as racist. (It should be noted that both my parents were members of the Eureka Chapter of the NAACP.) I don't think we went to any chamber music concerts after that.

My father set up a hi-fi system to replace the ancient console we'd lugged down from Seattle. He ordered a Heathkit amplifier and a Collaro Conquest record changer with a brush on the end of the tone arm like a little cowcatcher. He built a pair of speaker cabinets from kiln-dried redwood. They had oval cutouts and looked like huge boxes of Kleenex. Now all we lacked were long playing records, and we soon found them at Safeway, a twenty-four record set called *The Basic Library of the World's Greatest Music*. Each record came in a hinged cardboard box with a stitched-in booklet describing the composers and their works, and each booklet had its own sophisticated color. I didn't read the booklets because the type was too small, but the colors made me feel a bit like an adult.

The set should have been called *Nineteenth Century Western Music You Can Whistle To*. It included the war-horse piano concertos of Chopin, Tchaikovsky, Rachmaninoff and Grieg; symphonies by Beethoven, Brahms and Dvorak; and *The Nutcracker Suite* and *The Sorcerer's Apprentice*. The records were sequenced so that you could stack them up and play a complete work without flipping any of them over. My mother's favorite was Chopin's First Piano Concerto. Mine was Bach's Concerto for Two Violins followed by Vivaldi's Concerto for Two Trumpets, all eminently suitable for whistling.

My father began buying individual record albums, mostly organ music. He also bought a Mario Lanza record in RCA Victor Living Stereo. He left it near a window and it warped from the heat. This was awkward because my father often told us there was no such thing as an accident. He tried to flatten the record—sandwiched it between boards, weighted it down and put it back in the sun—but the damage was irreversible. I was discreetly pleased, first to witness his chagrin, and then because I didn't like Mario Lanza.

My piano teacher in Arcata was to be Charlie

Moon, a music department professor who gave private lessons to the sons and daughters of his colleagues after he was done teaching for the day. He was a tall man with huge hands and feet and teeth. Some said, sotto voce, that he was a *confirmed bachelor*. He could never get my name right. "Now, Clanton," he would begin in his Oklahoma drawl, and then he'd crack up. "Oh, my Gawd! I did it agayin." And he'd slap his forehead and his thigh and start over. Charlie told my parents, no doubt with good intentions, that I showed promise at the keyboard. What he might have added was that I didn't complement that promise with enthusiasm or discipline. And what he surely knew was that I practiced each day as carefully as I brushed my back molars. I set the timer for thirty minutes, played while it ticked and stopped immediately when it rang. I learned wrong notes as thoroughly as right ones and played both with indifference. I never truly understood musical notation and often navigated by ear. It never occurred to me that Artur Rubenstein was revered not just because he hit all the right keys, but because he touched them as he would touch a baby's cheek, or hammered them like a blacksmith. He made music. I played notes. But, then, I didn't want to be Artur Rubenstein. That said, I did ask to learn a few pieces I'd heard and liked—they eventually included Chopin waltzes and Polonaises, Beethoven's *Moonlight Sonata* and one of Debussy's *Arabesques*—and Charlie, nursing motivation where he could find it, said yes if he thought I could handle the level of difficulty without frustration.

My father bought me a new piano—a reconditioned 1902 Steinway baby grand—to go with my new teacher. This man who got invoices from a local hardware store addressed to *Orval Wholesale*, who hadn't driven a new car in my lifetime, wrote a check for $2,600 for a piano with eighty-eight keys just like the piano we already had. I imagine he was disappointed that it didn't help.

I had been taking piano lessons for about eight years when I started high school. My mother was proud of what she saw as my accomplishments, and sometimes asked me to play for guests. I never refused outright. I just squirmed and stared at my shoes until someone said, "No, no. Don't force him if he's not comfortable." At one point, Charlie encouraged me to learn a Haydn piano concerto well enough to play it with the college's student orchestra during rehearsals, but it didn't happen and I wasn't disappointed. More and more often, the first five or ten or even fifteen minutes of my weekly piano lesson would be a conversation unrelated to music. Charlie would laugh and give me hugs that nearly pulled me off his lacquered piano bench. He knew I was stalling and he played along.

I was afraid to tell my father that I wanted to quit taking lessons. I had hoped he would come up with the idea on his own, but he didn't. Not even after I sat sobbing on my bed after I'd been cut from the freshman basketball team because I had to practice arpeggios instead of lay ups. Not even after I set the timer and played the same C major scale for half an hour. Finally, three months before the end of my senior year, I told Charlie I'd had it. Charlie understood—by now he was my therapist as much as my teacher—but my father was baffled. "Did Charlie make a pass at you?" he wanted to know, as if that were the only possible explanation for my small rebellion. He didn't speak to me for days.

When I was twelve and Kath was eleven, we each got a transistor radio for Christmas. Now both of us could listen to what we liked on the radio stations we could pick up in Humboldt County. I took my new radio to bed with me and listened to Les Crane's call-in show. I liked knowing that things were going on in the world even though our house was dark and quiet. I also began listening to San Francisco Giants baseball games, almost as much for the unhurried pace of the play-by-play as for the thrill of a Willie Mays home run. And soon I discovered KRED, the local rock'n'roll station. Much of the music I'd listened to up to that point, whether it was the *New World Symphony* or "Three Coins in a Fountain," was like paint pouring out of a can—thick and smooth. But the Top 40 songs on KRED, like "The Night Has a Thousand Eyes" and "I Saw Linda Yesterday," were more like popcorn popping. It was hard to sit still while I listened. And many of these songs were about girls—wanting and getting, wanting and not getting, getting and losing—themes now much on my mind, if only in theory.

During the transition from my last years at Jacoby Creek Elementary School to my first years at Arcata High, the music I listened to evolved from *stealing a kiss* to *copping a feel*. I missed the sweetly earnest *Meet the Beatles*, but *Surrealistic Pillow* was a better match to my adolescent anxiety. I began to hear live rock'n'roll at after game dances in the high school gymnasium, and at the Lemon Tree, Arcata's teenage nightclub, which occasionally presented Bay Area bands and once brought in the Yardbirds to play a twenty minute set. I took comfort in the overwhelming noise and the concealing darkness, but I preferred the recorded versions of "Little Girl" and "Over Under Sideways Down" to the ragged live performances I'd heard. I wanted to anticipate the hooks and the choruses, knowing that when they came they would please me just like they did the last time I'd heard them.

I continued to listen to classical music. I often spent time in the college library researching debate topics, and while I was there I sometimes checked out records. I made a few discoveries, like Leos Janacek's *Sinfonietta* and Manuel de Falla's Concerto for Harpsichord and Five Instruments, but they were no match for the Byrds.

My years at UC Berkeley were lean ones. I didn't have a car, I rarely ate out and I bought my shirts on sale. But less than a week after I began my freshman year, I walked to Dale Sanford's TV and Hi-Fi on Shattuck Avenue, paid $250 for a portable stereo and carried it a mile and a half back to the dorm. There were stereos in many of the rooms on my floor, and most of them broadcast the same Cream and Jimi Hendrix and Steve Miller albums without mercy, but there were pockets of diversity. Mitch said dramatically that Edith Piaf's voice was exquisite, and he could pronounce Francoise Hardy's name more or less correctly. Rolf, across the hall, listened to all sorts of unfamiliar music. We called him Beethoven because he couldn't talk about Rudolf Serkin's interpretation of the Third Piano Concerto without fluttering his eyebrows and sighing. He tried to coax us into sharing his passion for Ravi Shankar and Donovan (who was by then writing songs about starfish), but he had better luck promoting Buffy Sainte-Marie. Rolf and I went to see Buffy at the Berkeley Community Theater. She Indian-walked to the microphone, unleashed her fearsome vibrato, whanged on a Jew's harp and did some wonderful costume changes. I died a little when Rolf told me that she lived with her boyfriend in Hawaii.

I began to notice the lyrics of gifted songwriters like Joni Mitchell and Randy Newman and Paul Simon. I thought of a few lines as aphoristic: *The love you take is equal to the love you make, Every form of refuge has its price* or *She thinks of the ocean as rivers set free*. But mostly I saw the words as subordinate to the music. I looked forward to the choruses of all those Motown girl group hits, the backup singers' *shoops* and *doops* of pure harmony. And I thought that symphonies and concertos advanced the principle a step further by omitting voices altogether, so that grand sweeps of musical expression wouldn't be polluted by words. There was no place for opera in my world.

I didn't thank my father for the twelve years I spent

fidgeting at the keyboard, but I did acquire some basic knowledge by osmosis. I learned about tonality and key and intervals and chords. I took several music appreciation classes at Berkeley, though they focused more on historical development than on the structure and character of particular compositions. Nineteenth century Romanticism was my turf. I wasn't interested in the trouvères and sinfonias that preceded it, or the frantic search for uniqueness of expression that eventually followed. I wanted to understand the workings of a Brahms symphony. What was it that drew me to Brahms and not to Schumann or Liszt? I scanned the commentaries on record jackets looking for clues, but here too I would encounter mostly historical context, and tedious pedantry to boot. I didn't give a fig about the composer's patrons, or the lakeside cottage where he wrote during the summer, or the hidebound critics who savaged the first public performances of his works. What fascinated me was how a melodic phrase or even a fragment of three or four notes, introduced early on, would pop up again and again, sometimes stated directly, sometimes modified, sometimes disguised so cleverly by syncopation or altered harmony that it could go unnoticed for many listenings. I marveled at the ingenuity of these devices. I wanted to congratulate myself for figuring them out and I became annoyed when I couldn't find supporting evidence.

Early on, I knew all too well that music could be performed skillfully or poorly. But because virtually all the music I listened to was recorded, it hadn't occurred to me that music can be performed *differently*. Each time I listened to my recording of Rubenstein playing Brahms's Second Piano Concerto, it was, not surprisingly, the same. Imagine my surprise when I first heard it performed live. *Wait a minute*, I thought. *That's not what Brahms meant. It's too fast or too slow or the horns are too loud.* This happened whenever I heard a familiar piece at a concert, and I thought it increasingly odd that I owned the only authentic version. I finally figured it out. Conductors and orchestras don't merely perform music, they interpret it, like actors playing *Macbeth*. From that point on, I went to the symphony to hear a familiar piece because of the unique interpretation and not in spite of it.

My concert-going experience has confirmed that no investment in amplifiers, preamps, subwoofers and gold-plated speaker cables can replicate the character of a live performance. Not just the ripe phrases of the cellos or the sparkle of the piccolos, but the aura—the vibes—of two thousand music lovers facing the same direction with a common purpose. Some people fiddle with their programs or cough or fall asleep, but most of us enter a symphony hall in somewhat the same way we would enter a cathedral, with a kind of reverence and the hope that we will be blessed.

Why Great Violinists Are Seldom Elephants

The concert hall grows quiet
As the maestro strides to center stage
The lights grow dim, all eyes on him
He tugs a cuff and turns a page.

He scans the silent orchestra
He takes in each expectant face
The tin-eared coots with silver flutes
The walruses on double bass.

The panthers poised with English horns
(They're dressed in black; how elegant)
And stone-deaf loons with their bassoons
But not a single elephant!

The maestro raises his baton
The orchestra begins at once
They play a sprightly overture
But why without some elephants?

If mice can master clarinets
And pandas pound the tympani

Then what excuse to introduce
An elephantless symphony?

They couldn't play the harp it's true
Arpeggios would make them sneeze
And as for cellos, they'd do well
Except they have such pudgy knees.

The trumpet? There's a worthy thought
Gorillas play them every day
The piccolo is tricky, though
With trunks forever in the way.

Perhaps they'd like to strike the gong
No sharps or flats to learn and yet
They only know fortissimo
The maestro would be quite upset.

And should you still expect to see
An elephant on violin,
Don't laugh, it's true. They're ticklish, too
Especially beneath the chin.

Toy Stories IV:
Model Behavior

There were advantages to growing up on the shore of Lake Washington. We could paddle around in orange life jackets. We could fish for perch or chub from the end of our decrepit dock. We could watch the traffic on the water, from armadas of ducklings in our little inlet to cabin cruisers farther out. Occasionally, an unlimited hydroplane would roar past on a practice run. I was mesmerized by hydroplanes. When I heard one approaching, I ran down to the water to watch it race by with its long, white rooster tail arcing out behind. I especially liked the oscillating growl of the engine as the sponsons bounced and spanked over the waves.

A score of hydroplanes competed each summer during the Seattle Sea Fair. We couldn't see the races from our dock, but we sometimes watched them with our neighbors on their television. (My father didn't like televisions so we didn't have one.) I studied the OFFICIAL GOLD CUP REGATTA programs and knew most of the boats and their identifying numbers and colors: Miss Bardahl, U-40, Green with Yellow accents; Maverick, U-00, Gold, Red and White; and my favorite; Hawaii Kai III, U-8, Tropical Rose and Coral. I must have been dreaming one spring day when Miss Burien, U-4, Red and White, came roaring down the lake from the north, sputtered, slowed, went dead in the water and slowly drifted up to our dock. My mother and I met the driver as he climbed from the cockpit. Could he use our phone, he wanted to know. I was speechless. I'd never been anywhere near Miss Burien, or any other hydroplane, and now here she was, curved and smooth and much bigger than I would have imagined.

My father noted my enthusiasm for hydroplanes and bought a scale model kit of Miss Thriftway, U-60, Mahogany, Cream, Orange and White, so we could build it together. The kit consisted of a box of die-cut sheets of balsa wood and some decals. My father did the building and I did the watching, and that was fine. It was our first such project together, and I was pleased that he had chosen to spend the time with me. He assembled Miss Thriftway piece by piece in short stretches between dinner and bedtime. The fitting and gluing and sanding took patience, something I lacked, but it was fascinating to watch the gradual transformation from the first ribs and blocking to the completed model. My father applied the striped decals to the hull, laid down coats of golden shellac and dropped in the tiny engine, but we never took the boat down to the lake and fired it up. I kept it in my bedroom for years and then gave it to a neighborhood playmate.

I assembled a few simple model airplanes when I was eight or nine, but I was a couple years older before I'd peeled enough cement from my fingers to qualify as a hobbyist, and by then I was only interested in 1:25 scale model cars sold as AMT 3 in 1 Customizing Kits. An unassembled kit cost $1.49 and came in a box the size of a loaf of bread. There were options: Build it Stock. Build it as a Beautiful Custom. Build it for the Track or Strip.

My first two AMTs were a '61 Imperial and a '62 Lincoln Continental. I have no idea why I chose these particular cars, but I built them Custom, meaning I glued the standard custom parts together as the instructions directed. Then I got serious with a '62 Chevy convertible. I used a brush to paint the body a gaudy nail polish red, and upholstered the seats with dark blue velour. The upholstery looked sharp, but the brush marks didn't, so I bought a can of spray paint for my next project, a '63 Mercury Monterey. I chose metal flake burgundy and, as instructed, I shook the can for a full minute before spraying. I painted the chassis and the engine compartment flat black and the engine block red. I ran lengths of black thread from the distributor to the cylinder heads. I didn't know what a distributor was or why it should be connected to the cylinders, but I'd seen thread used this way on some of the models my classmates brought to school.

The Mercury took first place in a contest at a local hobby shop. I was proud of my cheesy trophy, which was, I assume, an incentive to buy more model kits and spray paint. I built a pair of AMT '40 Fords—the sedan and the coupe—and I was working on a Revell '57 Chevy with doors that you could open when I entered high school, a new world where model makers were not held in high regard. I put the Chevy, painted but unassembled, back in its box, and put the box in the back of a closet.

Ex-smoker

Be brave, little cigarette
And guide me through the nighttime brambles

ERIC PURSER, TWO GRADES BEHIND ME AT ARCATA HIGH, wrote this fine poem. I remember it because I was a smoker for fifteen years and cigarettes were my faithful companions. I didn't have many companions as I endured my adolescence. At 5'9" I weighed 127 pounds. I wore glasses and braces and hated them both, just as I hated my curved nose and weak chin and unmanageable hair. I wasn't a dork or a spazz, but they were my first cousins. The taunts of a few of my classmates trailed after me for years.

What I wanted all through high school was to be dealt a fresh hand. I wanted straight teeth instead of straight As. I wanted a varsity jacket. I would have given anything to strut into the crowd at an after game dance knowing that I'd be admired and resented, but the only thing that I shared with the mesomorphic lettermen I admired and resented was an unrelenting hormonal tension.

I didn't start smoking to impress the girls with cheerful breasts and shining hair. As far as I knew, they didn't smoke. What I wanted to say to the world was *Please don't see me as I see myself.* I must have known that a skinny kid with braces and a cigarette was still a skinny kid with braces, but I had to strike out, at least symbolically, against my lot. And I knew, though I didn't plan to tell them, that my parents would disapprove, particularly my father, who expected me to rise above peer pressure, if not to transcend adolescence altogether.

Technically speaking, my parents were both smokers, although my father lit up only to blow smoke rings, which he did very well and not very often. My mother smoked four cigarettes a day, one after each meal and one with her evening glass of sherry. But she didn't inhale. She just pulled the smoke into her mouth, held it briefly, and blew it back out. She took her Pall Mall 100s out of the pack and kept them in a pewter creamer next to her favorite chair. One day, I retrieved an empty pack from the wastebasket—she never crumpled them—and began to refill it with cigarettes from the creamer, one at a time, for several weeks. What surprises me now is not that I didn't simply duck into Hutchins's Market to buy a pack of my own— I knew the FBI would be waiting to arrest me—but that I waited until I had a full pack before I tried to smoke one.

If God had it all to do over again, I'm betting She'd

reconsider tobacco and give us another variety of rose or an incurable strain of athlete's foot according to Her mood. Could anyone doubt that that first lungful and the reeling dizziness and nausea that followed were bad news? And the taste—the flavor, to use the marketing term—surely *that* couldn't be the motivation for lighting ten or twenty small fires a day. I meant to suggest aloof sophistication, not make myself sick.

On occasional Friday nights I rode around with other outcasts who didn't have dates, or hadn't been invited to an A-list party, or weren't parked somewhere out in the foggy darkness trying to coax the panty girdles off girls who would say no and mean yes. We sulked, burned rubber at traffic lights, and eventually drove to the Denny's on Fifth Street in Eureka, where we drank a little coffee with our cream and sugar, and smoked cigarettes.

Life improved after I graduated from high school. Those straight As got me a summer job as an engineering student trainee on a Caltrans survey crew, and the job got me out of the house. The crew's principal task that summer was to map the topography for several miles along the south side of Del Norte County's remote and picturesque Smith River in anticipation of someday turning two lanes into four. My primary role would be to clear brush with a bolo knife, but I also set a transit rod and held the dumb end of a metal tape measure. My coworkers were rednecks of a sort, not at all like my father and his colleagues at Humboldt State. They had banged up fingers and wore sweat-soaked shirts and put in a fair day's work as they intoned their well-worn complaints about niggers on welfare and the Pink Ears—the pale bureaucrats with clip-on ties who rarely left their air conditioned offices in Sacramento. My coworkers judged me only on the basis of my willingness to try. They were quietly amused when I winced at their rote bigotry. I liked them.

Almost to a man, they smoked. Not Pall Mall 100s, but stubby, filter-free Lucky Strikes and Camels. Les Spinney, the rummy crew chief, sat in the shade with a cigarette in one hand and a pencil in the other, neatly writing down the elevations as they were called out, and picking shreds of tobacco off his tongue with his thumb and forefinger. Al Randall sharpened his bolo knife with a file, squinting as the smoke from his lip-clenched Camel drifted up into his eyes. We used a rowboat to cross the river on our way to and from our survey line, and one morning Al mistimed his exit move at the far shore, plunging cursing and laughing into clear green water up to his neck. His clothes were soaked and so were his wallet and his only pack of cigarettes, freshly opened for a smoke or two with his breakfast coffee. I watched as he carefully tore the paper and foil away from these bedraggled cigarettes and lined them up on a flat rock to dry in the ninety-five degree heat until lunch. When he was through, he laid his damp driver's license and folding money next to them.

At some point during this strenuous and oddly peaceful summer, the housing office at UC Berkeley sent me a questionnaire so they could pair me with a compatible dormmate. I was now smoking daily, but I checked the nonsmoker box because I didn't yet think of *smoker* as one of my defining characteristics, like *left-handed* or *thin*. When I met my dormmate in September, I wished immediately that I had taken the question more literally. Earl, a genuine nonsmoker, was 6'5," with the stooped posture of someone who dearly wishes to be shorter. His huge hands dangled at his sides as though uncertain of their purpose. His voice ranged from a phlegmy rumble to a squeak. *Good Lord,* I thought. *What are they trying to tell me here?* Earl wasn't pleased, either. He hated the smell of stale smoke in his sheets and towels, and he opened the windows—or pushed them open wider—when he returned from his classes. Like all smokers, I had a dulled sense of smell, and thought he was simply being petulant. Sorry, Earl. I owe you one.

I continued to smoke Pall Malls and then switched to Tareytons. I smoked a pipe for awhile. Eventually, I became a Marlboro Man. I'm sure I was swayed by the square-jawed cowboys I saw on billboards, but what closed the deal was the simple red and white packaging and the durability of the flip-top box. A conventional pack could take a beating in the pocket of my pea coat, but the box kept my cigarettes intact. It also held up well when I tamped it against my palm to pack the tobacco so it would burn slower. I tried the stylish imports I saw some of my classmates smoking—English Ovals, Export A, Player's Cut. I even bummed the odd Gauloises, but its harsh smoke slammed into the back of my throat like a Citroën with failed brakes. To survive finals week, I drank Coke and smoked Kools one after another until my moustache glistened with tar. One summer I even rolled my own with Bugler's tobacco, which burned as fiercely as Topanga Canyon in a dry year. But I always came back to Marlboros, three quarters of a pack a day.

During my last year in grad school, I'd come to acknowledge that I wasn't a smoker solely by choice. It was a dismal year: I spent the afternoons puttering un-productively at my desk in Wurster Hall, then went back to my room and lay on the bed, watching television and filling my ashtray until all the stations were off the air except an all-night movie channel hosted by a waterbed salesman. I slept twelve hours a day. But depressed though I was, I began to fret about the cartons of cigarettes I paid for—like my monthly phone bill— without question. I switched to Merit, a brand with about half the tar and nicotine as my companions from Marlboro Country. And companions they had become.

I understood that friendship is conditional, that friends aren't always home when you call, that they might not want to hear one more time that you feel like crying and don't see the point of it all. But I could light a cigarette as often as I needed to. I could feel the smoke hit my throat and lungs. It wasn't a lover's caress, but it was a kind of touch. And every exhalation was a long sigh.

My spirits improved after I finally graduated. I free-lanced briefly and then went to work for an employer who disliked smoking intensely and didn't allow it in his office. His prohibition assured me five opportunities a week to survive a day without nicotine. There was no time to smoke as I rushed off to work in the morning, and it didn't seem worth the bother to smoke at lunchtime, so I only smoked in the evenings and on weekends. By now every cigarette was simply a concession to habit and lack of will. I knew that with each sulfurous stink of a struck match and each morning's wad of phlegm I was slowly whittling down my life expectancy. I began to buy packs instead of cartons. I tried to quit several times, but I could only hold out for a day or two, and then my first cigarette would make me dizzy, reminding me instantly why I had tried so hard not to smoke it.

After smoking Merits for several years, I switched to Carltons, or Carltoons, as they were known to anyone who tried to suck anything at all—tar, nicotine, smoke, taste—through their dense filters. I compensated by cutting the filter in half, but, filter or not, the companionship of a Carlton brought little satisfaction or comfort. And so here, finally, was a reason to quit—that there was no longer a compelling reason to continue. I had a few friends by now, and a career of sorts, and interests—landscape photography, writing, exploring mountain wilderness. To quit after years of trying and failing would be a life-affirming accomplishment.

It happened unexpectedly. I'd gone up to Lake Tahoe on a ski trip with three nonsmoking friends and left my Carltons at home. We skied on Saturday, but it snowed all night and it was still snowing Sunday morning, so we headed back to the Bay Area. The trip, normally about four hours, took fourteen thanks to blizzard conditions and a couple of jackknifed big rigs. When I finally made it to bed, I could feel a cold coming on. I didn't smoke when I had a cold because it only made things worse. When my head cleared enough for me to think about it, I realized that I hadn't had a cigarette for almost a week. I was surprised and then elated and then anxious. If I couldn't quit now, would I ever be able to?

But I stayed with it. Friends who'd quit before me cheered me on. Friends who still smoked urged me to set a good example. The craving fought hard for attention at times, but each day without a cigarette brought a little more pride and required a little less will. I promised myself two things. First, that I would never succumb to curiosity and *try just one*. And second, that if I ever fell off the wagon, I'd smoke real cigarettes. To die from lung cancer after smoking Carltons would be inexcusable.

I smoked for fifteen years, and it's now been well more than thirty since I ground out my last butt. Attitudes about smoking have changed a great deal since then, and now that smokers have been systematically shooed from the public realm, I have to remind myself that cigarettes once smoldered unremarkably nearly everywhere. My pediatrician smoked. My high school German teacher made key-jingling sprints to the teacher's lounge for a few quick drags between classes. Smokers smoked in grocery stores and movie theaters and in line at the post office. They—we—smoked on Greyhound buses and in doctors' waiting rooms. During the slow transition to smoke-free hospitals and restaurants and offices, I was a self-righteous ex-smoker. I grew livid at the thought that anyone should have the right to pollute my lungs after my long struggle to stop polluting them myself.

I should have more compassion for smokers, especially the ones who've been at it for decades and may die an awful death as a result. Many seem aggrieved and forlorn, except for the sullen teenage smokers slumped artfully just beyond No Smoking zones at building entrances. I know what they're up to, and to a degree I admire them because they look vaguely ominous in a way I'm sure I never did. If I thought they'd be willing to take my experience into consideration, I'd worry that they were losing their touch, but this is what I would tell them if they asked: Years after my last cigarette, I still dreamed that I'd started to smoke again and wouldn't be able to stop.

Penelope Poems

Penelope pokes at her waffle
She says Mommy this waffle is awful
Her mother, unkind
Says I'll smack your behind
Penelope says that's unlawful.

Penelope ponders her pancakes
The pancakes her grandmother
Anne makes
She says Granny, in Europe
They serve them with syrup
But Indians eat them with bran flakes.

Penelope's passion is porridge
In fact, it's her favorite forage
She slurps it on Sunday
But Monday's the one day
She doesn't, because it's in storage.

Penelope peddles papayas
With poise and aplomb, and yet try as
She might, recent sales have been

slight, save to bankers
and portly pariahs.

Penelope pampers Amanda
(Amanda's Penelope's panda)
She adds fresh bamboo
To a faux bamboo stew
And serves it with faux jacaranda.

DREAM JOURNAL

IN MY DREAMS, REMEMBERING is a sometime thing. I remember my college years, but apparently I'm as absent-minded as any professor. I sign up for a class, forget about it until finals week and then panic. I haven't been to class or cracked a textbook because I don't know what class it is or who teaches it or where it's being taught. I need to find a course catalog to see if anything looks familiar, but I've forgotten where they hand them out. I rush to the student union, but they don't have any, so I run to Sproul Hall, and they don't have any either...

I can't find my car. I parked it on one of the side streets near campus, taking a moment to fix the location in my mind so I'll recognize it when I come back after class, but I forget anyway. It's nearly dark when I begin searching, walking down one likely block after another, ranging farther and farther from the university into a neighborhood where I don't feel safe. At last, I see it from a distance, partially hidden by another car. My steps quicken and I begin to relax, but it isn't my car after all...

I can't find my dorm room. I make it to the right dormitory and sometimes I sense I'm on the right floor and even that my room should be close to the elevator, but the numbers on the doors aren't in any logical sequence as I walk back and forth along the dimly lighted corridor. Or it's the first day of my freshman year and I've found my room but there are already two people in it.

As an adolescent, I had rare flying dreams in which I extended my arms and soared weightless beneath the ceiling in the Arcata High gymnasium. Jumping dreams were more common. I would run a few steps to build up speed and then take unbelievably long, effortless strides, barely touching down on the balls of my feet. I didn't rise far above the ground, but I could neutralize gravity and extend each stride as long as I wanted.

I dreamed about an amazing pond in the woods behind our house. Kath and I and the neighbors' kids often played in these woods, a complicated tangle of standing and toppled trees and upturned stumps of old growth redwoods. But there was no pond there during the day, only at night when I dreamed about it—a small, shallow pool of clear water filled with fish and brightly colored salamanders crawling slowly along the bottom.

If I'd been one of Freud's analysands, he would have found it more difficult to argue that dreams are about wish fulfillment. I had the bathroom dream, again, Herr Doktor. I walk into the men's room at work with, you know, The Urge, but all the toilet stalls are occupied, and then everyone's gone but the place is a horror. All the toilets are overflowing and the wet floor is covered with turds and wads of toilet paper. What do you think this means, Herr Doktor? But Freud just looks at me and strokes his beard.

I've also dreamed about landslides. Each one begins as a small trickle of rock and dust down a mountain on the opposite side of a valley. Sometimes I hear it before I see it. I watch as it grows bigger and louder, dislodging boulders the size of teakettles, garbage cans, Lincoln Continentals, until whole slabs of mountain are breaking loose. The boulders careen and thunder down into the valley and out across it. Then they begin to bounce up toward me—far below me, and then not so far, and then not far at all...

Some of my dreams occur in the houses where I grew up. I'm rummaging through the closet in my bedroom and I find a dozen stylish shirts and pairs of pants I didn't know I had, but I wake up before I can try them on. Or it's raining at night and I see a leak and then another one. Water is streaming into the house, and the floor is rotten and collapsing. There's no safe place for me to walk.

The jet fighter attack happens near the house. I see an enormous military aircraft approaching, then more and more of them until a great armada is droning overhead. Something's up, I think, but then the armada is gone and a single jet—an F-15, maybe—comes in much closer from another direction. I duck reflexively into the trees, but it circles closer. I've been spotted. The jet looms, grazes the treetops, hovers. The pilot locks eyes with me. Abruptly, he climbs with impossible speed and loops around to hurtle straight down, piercing the ground at my feet with the plane's nose. Once, twice, three times, *Bap! Bap! Bap!* like a harrowing outsize game of mumblety-peg.

I once had a Jungian therapist with bad '50s paintings on her office walls and a flatulent Corgi at her feet. One afternoon, I told her about a remarkable dream I'd had soon after my father died: I've walked to his office on the Humboldt State campus to catch a ride home after school. I find him sitting at his desk in his coat and tie, but his head is missing. In its place, tucked neatly into his collar, is a cylindrical clear glass bowl filled with water. In the bowl, underwater, is a neatly coiled black snake. *What does this mean?* I asked.

She shrugged.

Tide Pool Healthcare
I. The Toothache

A lobster phoned her dentist
In extraordinary haste.
You've got to treat me right away
We haven't time to waste.

I think I've lost a filling
And there's little I can chew.
I'm sick of mashed potatoes
Is there something you can do?

Her dentist weighed his options
And he spoke with trusted friends.
He thumbed through recent journals
And he charted recent trends.

He tugged his ear, he tapped his chin
He rubbed his tummy, too.
And then he slapped his forehead
He was certain what to do.

He jotted down his findings
And he tucked them in a folder.

He called his ailing patient back
And this is what he told her:

I must confess I've very little
Wisdom to bequeath.
But how can you have a toothache
When you haven't any teeth?

But Not For Me

IT WAS A BALMY SPRING DAY, and my friend, Dave, and I were enjoying the afternoon sunshine on the deck of the South Campus rooming house where we lived. We talked for hours about all sorts of things. At one point Dave said, *Of course we'll both be getting married and raising families.* I nodded, but for me there was no such certainty. Getting married was not something you did as a matter of course, like paying taxes or getting your teeth cleaned, and there was nothing about my parents' marriage that made me want to have one of my own. Their day-to-day relationship was matter of fact, verging on rote. They mostly spoke to each other when they needed to. They hugged occasionally, but kissed rarely, at least when my sisters and I were around.

When I watch friends nuzzle their children, cherish them, reason with them beyond the point of exasperation, I can't understand why my parents were so detached. My mother told me that she had divorced her first husband in part because he was indifferent to their daughter, Judy. She told me that my father said he wanted a dozen children, yet there were times when he seemed overwhelmed by the bitterness he felt toward just one of them. When I was nine, I remember reaching up to take his hand as we walked out of a Chinese restaurant in Eureka. I was a little embarrassed—I thought I was too old—but I liked the feel of his warm fingers. It was a novel sensation because we rarely touched.

I was often sick until my tonsils came out. My mother would touch me like a nurse, gently pressing her palm to my forehead to check for fever. She bathed Kath and me in the kitchen sink and sang "Rockabye Baby" or "Mockingbird Hill" as she toweled us dry and hugged us, but these were special moments. Until we were old enough for school, Kath and I relied on each other for company. My mother cooked and cleaned and gardened. She read the newspaper and talked to her friends on the phone. My father taught during the day and graded papers in the evening. Neither got down on hands and knees to join us in our childhood world. Certainly there were happy moments, like looking for Easter eggs among my mother's brightly colored flower gardens, or suffering through dinner on Christmas Eve so we could open our presents, or smearing homemade boysenberry jam on French toast on a Sunday morning. There was humor, too, and even enthusiasm, but joy was unknown territory.

Anger was not. My father was easily irritated and prone to hold a grudge. He could retract for days, withholding not only his affection—which might be difficult to notice—but any form of communication at all. Sometimes I was happy I didn't have to deal with him for awhile, but my mother couldn't handle these withdrawals because they played too directly on her insecurities. She hadn't graduated from high school, and she was married to a college professor with a PhD.

Both of our parents swatted us a few times. I wasn't afraid of my mother and her wooden yardstick, but my father was another story. He gave me just one formal spanking when I was about six, a classic wait-'til-your-father-gets-home nightmare. He wrestled me onto his lap, pulled down my pants and slapped me flesh against flesh. I looked up as I struggled against him and saw that he was grinning, amused by my effort to resist his overwhelming strength. I never forgave him for that, or for never once telling me that he was proud of me. Or that he loved me.

That I didn't imagine myself dating or going steady or marrying or becoming a parent may have been due, in part, to my parents' remoteness and lack of affection, but I believe that chronic self-gratification played a more important role. I was a precocious masturbator, beginning at the age of three or four. I was sleeping in a crib in my parents' bedroom then, shielded by a folding wooden screen. I remember moving carefully so the crib wouldn't squeak. From that time on, though I saw no sign that my parents disapproved or were even aware, though it would be years before my schoolmates smirked at rumors that one or another of us was jerking off, I became increasingly ashamed until, as an adolescent, I lived in a more or less continual state of low-grade mortification. *Because everyone knew.* I used that shame, in part, to justify my fear of dipping my toe into intersexual waters. I assumed other boys my age were just as flustered and awkward around girls as I was, but they still tried, however clumsily, to make productive use of their horniness, and some would say noisily that they had succeeded. I didn't try. It was as if I believed that being sexually active on my own disqualified me from being sexually active with anyone else. If I tried to unbutton a girl's blouse or slide my fingers under her skirt, if I acted as if I had the right to try, she would be repulsed. She would tell her friends and they would humiliate me without remorse. *Because they knew.*

Every year on their anniversary my father would give my mother a gardenia and sing "The Girl That I Marry" to her. That was their song. Here are a few of mine.

Eight Days a Week

One winter I ran from the school bus each morning to be the first to make tiny snowballs from the thick frost on the seats of the swings at Jacoby Creek Elementary School. The next fall, I was a timid freshman on a high school campus with muscle cars in the parking lot, football players close to twice my size, and girls with breasts. It was bad enough that I had begun wearing glasses in grade school, but now I had braces, too, and not just braces, but one of those miniature crossbows that wrapped around my face like a relic from the Spanish Inquisition. I lost what little self-confidence I'd had. I began to hide inside a coat, first a green one with matted synthetic fur and then a navy pea coat. Sometimes I'd drape the coat over the back of my chair in a classroom, or sling it over my shoulder, but it was my security blanket and I wouldn't walk down the street without it. During lunch, unless I had a meeting to attend—Key Club, Junior Statesmen, Model United Nations—I'd retreat to the classroom that my favorite English teacher normally kept open. If the door was locked, I felt as if I'd run out of gas in a bad part of town.

I did my best to focus on world history and algebra, but horniness was never far away. I was very much aware of the girls in my classes—their shapes, their complexions, whether they dressed well or poorly, how they moved. I catalogued them without pity as desirable or sexless or repugnant. But even though I had little regard for myself or anyone else, and in spite of the sarcastic comments I dished out without editing, there were a few girls, even *desirable* ones, who were aware of me, too. Pauline, a clear-eyed, playful sophomore—an older woman—stretched a lean leg across the aisle in speech class to pull one of my socks down with her toe. She asked me to the Sadie Hawkins dance and I happily accepted. I assumed we would get hitched and wear plastic wedding rings for a week just like our classmates. But then I heard that—no surprise—it was customary for Sadie and L'il Abner to kiss before they slid on their rings. I'd never kissed a girl, and my stomach tightened at the thought of fumbling at it in public. I went to the dance with Pauline, but when she suggested that we pay a visit to Marryin' Sam, I stared at the floor and mumbled an awkward demurral.

Cheryl and her family moved from the Midwest to Arcata during my sophomore year, and she and I were eventually attracted to each other in a tentative and halting way. She was wholesome and pretty and popular, and I took pride in walking her to class because it was like wearing that plastic wedding ring—it signified inclusion. We listened to music in her bedroom a few times and I took her to the junior prom, but she was beginning to sink into her own adolescent swamp and we were both too morose to become supporting friends and, maybe, sexual explorers.

The one girl I longed for from Freshman Honors English to graduation and beyond was Amanda Jensen. I was not alone. Half the boys in our class were carrying a torch for Amanda. She was the All Around Girl. She made honor role each quarter, sang in Madrigal, served in student government, and wore athlete's stripes on the sleeve of her black and orange school sweater. Amanda was cheerful without being annoying, and she seemed poised and serene when so many of us couldn't get comfortable in our skins. She dressed just a little more conservatively than most of the other girls, her skirts well-fitted but not tight, her colors richer and more subtle. I saw her as a member of a higher caste, but I wanted to be with her anyway because she sparkled, and because being with her would ensure that I, too, should be admired, that my sorry coming of age had been an injustice that would finally be set right.

I didn't ask Amanda out or tell her I found her attractive because I knew that as soon as I revealed my feelings she would pull back, and for me nothing could be worse than rejection, however gentle. I would in time endure frustration and depression and torment, become a cauldron of unhappiness that boiled over onto anyone patient enough to bear witness, but I wouldn't ask so that I wouldn't be rejected. So I was Amanda's friend. We talked occasionally, we slow danced once to the Beatles' "Eight Days a Week," and we were teammates on Arcata High's delegation to the Model United Nations in Berkeley. We cut class one morning and drove to Moonstone Beach in her family's bug-eyed Austin-Healey Sprite. I told her I'd been upset that things didn't work out with Cheryl.

After we graduated, Amanda went to school in Denmark for a year and I went off to Berkeley. We began to exchange letters, and after her first one arrived, I opened my mailbox at the dorm every day anxious to find the next one. When she wrote that she might visit me in Berkeley after she got back to the States, I kept watch for the bug-eyed Sprite. That summer, while my family spent two weeks at Pear Point, Amanda and her family would be sailing up the West Coast to Vancouver and passing close by. Stop and see us, I said. Maybe we can, she replied. I kept watch for a sailboat that never appeared, and while I was watching, Amanda was falling in love with a wealthy Canadian she had met. She told me when I called her at the end of the summer that she would soon be getting married.

THE BLACK ANGEL'S DEATH SONG

I began my tenure as a seasonal employee of the California Department of Parks and Recreation by working as a park aid at Humboldt Redwoods State Park, about four hours north of San Francisco on Highway 101. My first job there—arguably the best job I ever had—was to pick up litter all day on shaded trails beneath those redwoods. After I got off work, I ate a can of Dinty Moore Beef Stew and then sat outside sipping a beer and enjoying the warm evening. The other seasonal employees did much the same, and a couple teenagers whose parents worked at the park year-round sometimes joined us. One of them, Alice, was the sixteen-year-old daughter of the chief ranger. She was dark-skinned, slender, quiet and slightly knock-kneed, and when she wore tight white pants you could make out the floral pattern of her underwear. Alice often hung out with her friend, Sandra, and I sometimes joined them, sitting in the back row at a campfire program or playing ping pong in the rec room.

I suppose that Alice found me—one of those left-wing Berkeley types—to be somewhat exotic. One evening she sat on my lap nursing a can of Burgermeister, and a few evenings later she showed up for a visit on a day when my housemates were all somewhere else. We sat stiffly on the couch, looking like a Norman Rockwell cover for the *Saturday Evening Post*, Alice's hands folded in her lap, my arm draped casually over her shoulder like a stick of firewood, both of us staring straight ahead. Earlier, I'd been listening to Creedence Clearwater and Judy Collins, but when Alice arrived it was side two of the *Velvet Underground & Nico*. A more attentive host might have changed the music, but as it was we sat silently until "The Black Angel's Death Song" stopped screeching, and then she went home.

I moped around for a few days and then Alice invited me and two of my coworkers over for dinner with her parents. She served cake and ice cream in the living room and the five of us watched television. When it came time for me to get ready for the graveyard shift (I was now cleaning bathrooms in the wee hours instead of picking up trash in the forest) she led me out the back door so we would be alone when she looked up at the stars with her face tilted at a perfect kissing angle. That kiss, my first, may have been the purest, sweetest moment of my life. It was also the apex of a fledgling summer romance—Alice soon found one of the other park aids to be more interesting. The next summer, quite by chance, I saw her wedding announcement in the *Humboldt Times-Standard*.

FIRE AND RAIN

After one year in the dorms and two more in crowded living quarters off campus, I spent my senior year in a sunlit second floor apartment with Michael, a roommate who didn't consider a toilet brush a bourgeois affectation. No more tests of will to see who would be the first to give up and scrape moldy chili from dishes that had been stacked in the sink for a week.

Although Michael was an orderly housekeeper, he was also a world-class slob. I thought of him as a young Walter Matthau, tall, stooped and pale, wearing wrinkled shirts and scuffed shoes. He shuffled when he walked. He smoked constantly. He drooled while he slept, decorating his pillowcase with amoebic spit stains. Despite his slovenliness, Michael was a howling success with women. I watched in awe as he leaned out of our front window to chat with coeds passing by on the sidewalk below. "Hello. What have you got in there?" he asked a preppy blonde as she approached with a bag of groceries. "Eggs? Hey, that's great. We were going to bake some brownies, but we're out of eggs. Right, Stannie?"

Our neighbors in the apartment above were Jennifer

and Leslie, two freshmen from LA. We knew when they were back from class because they played James Taylor's "Fire and Rain" endlessly. Michael had long since been upstairs to borrow a cup of sugar, and he was patiently coaxing zaftig Jennifer away from her high school sweetheart. Soon, he was seeing a lot of her, and because he was a show-off and she was passively indulgent, I saw a lot of her, too. Michael and I would come home from Park'n'Shop with our week's supply of Tater Tots and frozen raspberry turnovers, he'd give Jennifer a call, and by the time I'd put the food away and gone into the living room to hand him his carton of Winstons, they'd be stretched out on his bed—it was a one bedroom apartment—with her sweater bunched up at her chin and her bell bottoms tugged down to her knees. Or I'd be reading the Sunday *Chronicle* in the bedroom, and Michael would yell, "Hey, Stannie. Come look at this." He'd bared Jennifer's ample breasts and sucked her nipples to full protrusion. He gave me a waggish grin as she regarded me drowsily.

Late one night, they were slapping and tickling, and I was awake when Jennifer walked nude past my bedroom on her way to the kitchen. It was the first time I'd seen all of her remarkable features at once, and as she walked back down the hall, I got out of bed and pranced nude behind her. The three of us sat on Michael's bed, twenty fingers tracing the contours of Jennifer's geography from every direction. "I feel like I'm being mauled," she said. I thought Michael and I were being very gentle.

Jennifer began field-testing her sexual allure, and the traffic of her suitors soon teased out the possessiveness beneath Michael's thin layer of charm. He stormed out of town with another coed one weekend and told me not to spill the beans, but that didn't square with my Howdy Doody ethic—or my envy—so I told Jennifer anyway. She was upset when she came downstairs that evening. She tried sleeping in Michael's bed, then crawled into mine. I stroked her smooth back and the sides of her breasts, discovering a pimple and mindlessly circling it with my finger because it was there. "Yep," she said. "That's a zit."

Jennifer had clearly become casual about sex, and I think she saw me as an underdog who deserved sympathy, maybe even a mercy fuck. One morning after Michael had left for campus and I was hunched over the coffee table finishing a scale model of a housing project, Jennifer stirred in his bed and stretched like a panther. "There's room for two," she said as she drew back the sheet. I flushed. "Gotta run," I blurted. "Don't want to be late for class."

IF I NEEDED YOU

By the time I was twenty-five, I had begun to see my life as a journey across a desert where no vaginal flowers bloomed. Then I met Marie. Marie Santucci, Emotional Dismantler, she would claim, though she wasn't that ambitious. She could happily spend an afternoon sunbathing in the nude, watching her orange cats lick their bottoms spotless.

I was working for a man named Charley at the time. Marie was a friend of Charley's wife, Natalie, and Natalie had invited Marie to an open house across the courtyard from Charley's office. It was a typical white wine and Brie gabfest, and I would have soon left if I hadn't begun playing ping pong with Marie. She attacked the ball with more force than precision and then chased it down in the potted plants behind me, grazing me with her breasts each time she inched past. She apparently wanted my attention, and I was happy to give it. We played until it was too dark to play anymore and then we talked. That is, I talked. Marie brayed, shrieked, mugged. Words didn't flow from her mouth, they ran for their lives. *D'ya know what I mean?* she would demand, brows arched, eyes bugged, hands assailing the space between us. *D'ya know what I mean?* It was love at first collision.

Later, I told Natalie that I thought Marie was hot,

and Natalie, prone to mischief, tucked me into a dinner gathering at Ramona's Mexican restaurant along with Charley and Marie and Marie's lover Carlos and someone named Edgar, who had once been Marie's lover and would soon be Natalie's. *I'll have the chicken enchiladas with green sauce*, I said. Marie, who had been dressed casually when I first met her, was wearing a crisp white blouse with black slacks, and her blond hair, freed from its ponytail, flowed grandly over her shoulders. It would have been easy to admire her from a distance because she was living with Carlos, and even easier to be intimidated by her brassy aura. Instead, I saw her as vulnerable and approachable because she had a mouthful of braces just like the ones I'd worn in high school.

I called Natalie the next day. It was a long conversation because all conversations with Natalie were long, but I told her in essence that I wanted Marie, and she suggested in essence that I go for it. Then she called Marie and recapped the conversation. When the phone was no longer busy, I called Marie and asked her to lunch. She accepted. She wore a bright floral sundress and told me that she intended to be faithful to Carlos, but we talked for three hours and she was clearly flattered by my attention. She'd been hit on by most of the auto mechanics in San Rafael, but a designer who talked about books was new territory. Our lunch conversation initiated what may have been the longest foreplay ever conducted by two people beyond the age of consent.

Marie came to the house in the Oakland Hills where Dave and I had moved after we left the rooming house in Berkeley. She and I sat on the deck and talked and chain smoked until my hands trembled. I was almost sick with tension when she left.

We lolled in meadow sunshine above the house she shared with Carlos, and I asked if it would be OK to feel her breasts, a request she was probably hearing for the first time. I nuzzled her ear in a parking lot. *There's something I need to ask you*, I said. *Do you have a magnificent bush?* She hadn't heard that one either. I unfastened her halter top under a street light on a warm evening. I lifted her dress and cupped her slick-pantied buttocks as we kissed and swayed in her driveway. We sat in her parked Volkswagen and I combed my fingers through her pubic hair while people in the apartment building next to us loaded their dishwashers. If Marie had been as direct as Jennifer, I would probably have panicked and bolted, but whether she was sensitive to my emotions or merely curious, she allowed me to learn the shapes and textures of her body, and I became hungry instead of fearful. I was, finally, doing what I assumed my high school classmates had been doing a dozen years before.

I worked ten-hour days Wednesday through Saturday, so I could visit Marie early in the week while Carlos was selling auto parts. She wanted to be a country western singer—it was her one ambition beyond being provided for—and she was good. I remember walking to her door thinking I heard Emmylou Harris singing "If I Needed You," but the voice and guitar broke off abruptly when I knocked. Marie sang with her eyes closed, not because she was self-conscious—she certainly wasn't—but to narrow her focus. The richness of her voice made my scalp tingle, and the nearness of her body made me eager to touch. She was a ferocious racquetball player, and her full thighs were smooth and powerful. To me they were womanly, just as her prominent nose was a fitting counterpart to her strong cheekbones, but she saw herself as unladylike and coarse.

Marie was as direct and unpretentious lying nude on the living room floor as she was sorting socks at the laundromat. She showed me a photograph Carlos had taken while she was giving him a blow job. She told me that the surest way to arouse her was to rake my fingernails lightly over her thighs and ass. She said I'd know when I got it right because she'd become very wet and smell like a fish market, and she was right on both counts. It gave me pleasure to touch her, and it gave me more when she bucked and groaned in response.

We drove to Arcata for Thanksgiving with my mother and Kath while Carlos flew to New Mexico to spend time with his daughter from a previous marriage. My mother had a long established policy that visiting couples could share the same bed only if they were married or had been cohabitating for at least seven years. I held my parents partly responsible for the fact that my virginity had survived the Sexual Revolution, and I suggested, with some force, that my mother grant me an exemption. We compromised. Marie and I could sleep in the same bed provided we stayed on our respective sides of the mattress, which, more or less, we did.

This was the first Thanksgiving dinner without my father. Perhaps because my newfound intimacy with Marie had drawn my emotions closer to the surface, I thought about him and began to cry. I left the table and Marie followed. She didn't understand why I still felt sadness and suggested I get on with life. We continued to talk, and at some point—I felt then that it was important to say everything I thought to be true—I told her I didn't hear bells ringing when we were together. Marie curled into a fetal ball and wouldn't speak. I was stunned. I didn't believe I could cause anyone such pain. I wanted to take back my words and throw them into the ocean. I wanted to comfort Marie, but she wouldn't have it. And I thought, *Shit, I've just blown my chance to get laid.*

But Marie recovered, and we returned to the Bay Area a day before Carlos. She had decided that we would make love the following morning. She was, she said, a poor sleeper who generally insisted on sleeping alone, but on this occasion she agreed to share her bed rather than point me toward the cot by the front door where Carlos slept except for the two days a month when he was granted a conjugal visit.

The morning did not begin well. Marie's assessment: frisky but flaccid. I was puzzled more than chagrined. I'd been lusting for Marie for months. Why not now? Because it was wrong to transgress her relationship with Carlos, or because Marie's explicit consent dampened the thrill of transgression? Opening night jitters? Whatever the cause, I was on my own. Marie lay beside me while I tried, again and again, to coax an erection. One of her cats jumped onto the bed, fell asleep, woke up and jumped back down. Distant children shouted and laughed during recess. And still I tried. I couldn't let this opportunity pass. Marie, no doubt wondering just how long this was going to take, went into the bathroom to get hand lotion. She squatted next to me on the bed, poured out a generous puddle, and began vigorously rolling my penis between her palms like an abuela shaping tortillas. That didn't work either, but I will always cherish the image—Marie frowning in concentration, her tongue between her lips as it probably was when she was learning to subtract.

At last, after hours of effort, I rounded third base and slid home. Marie was hysterically grateful. I was emotionally spent and lightheaded from hunger. We had shared no obvious tenderness or affection, but Marie, as self-absorbed as I, had nevertheless found the patience to stay with me and receive me when I was finally ready. She was, on that morning, a saint.

We made love at my house a week later, but by now Marie had concluded that I was not the guy to take over the payments from Carlos, and she was ready to move on. She began hanging out with a rodeo cowboy who, she confided, had not only tongued her so skillfully that she came three times, but was content not to climb aboard afterward. And if he wasn't complaining, I shouldn't be either. But I was. I wrote her long, petulant letters. If I could no longer have her, I would at least convince her that I was right to feel aggrieved. Marie rose to the bait, and why not? She had little else to do. Our epistolary affair, as she called it, went on until I reluctantly acknowledged that she could offer her smooth brown body or withdraw it as she chose.

Not long after all this, Marie and Carlos left Marin for LA, where Marie left Carlos for the mechanic who worked on her Volkswagen. She returned to Marin and moved in with a welder who lived at the back of his shop. She was born again. She got married and moved with her new husband to a trailer park in Tennessee. Every year or so she calls her former lover, Edgar, usually after two or three glasses of wine. When I see Edgar, I ask him how she's doing. I'm always relieved to hear that she is, by some measure, doing OK.

SOMETHING BY MOZART

While Marie was leaving Carlos and the mechanic and the welder, Natalie left Charley for Edgar. Charley went ballistic for a month and then focused his considerable energy on seeing who else was out there. He ordered the biggest hot tub he could find and placed a personal ad in the *Bay Guardian*. It must have been a good one, because he got a slew of letters in response. One came with a topless photo. Another began *I am a tree spirit. I dance on the wind.* Charley was fascinated.

So was I. After my affair with Marie, I assumed I would move among women like a vegan in the produce section, but I soon lapsed into old habits and suffered the consequences. A personal ad seemed comparatively painless. I could communicate my intent without making eye contact, and know that the women who responded would be—in theory—unattached. I labored over my ad, word by word, until I felt it was suitably whimsical and distinct...

W/M, 31, designer and latent extrovert, seeks self-assured, independent, attractive, articulate woman, 25-35, as companion to share the middle ground between zipless encounters and a commitment carved in stone. I like Hunan lamb, armed snuggle, solitude, Rachmaninoff, mountains, Kermit the Frog, thunderstorms, Tom Wolfe, crisp collars, messy sandwiches, moonlight, Christmas, ladybugs, and a solid backbeat. I worked (hard) for John Anderson. I can be amusing, inspired and tender (and arrogant, insecure and surly before noon). Mail hand-written response and photograph to Guardian Box #9-E.

A score of responses arrived in the course of a month, most of them sincere and straightforward. Frances, for example, countered Rachmaninoff and Kermit the Frog with Woody Allen and artichoke quiche, a fatal mistake. Natasha didn't send a photo, rightly pointing that she didn't know what I looked like either. Mahalia wrote that she liked herself a lot except on the days when she didn't. Evelyn had a fat ass and good legs, or so she said, and someone named Susan wondered if I might be someone named Robert whom she had met in a previous life.

How to decide who to contact based on these one or two page letters, each as self-serving as my ad? I eliminated the earth mothers and astral voyagers, most of the responses without photographs, and all the women who showed no signs of vivacity or wit. That left Karla with a K, who needlessly apologized for being only twenty-four, looked scrumptious in a crisp, white dress, and wasn't interested in seeing me a second time; Carla with a C, a cuddly nurse who had added fifteen or twenty pounds to cuddle since her photo had been taken; Laura, close to catatonic; Annette, the sort of woman you ought to bring home to meet mother; and Priscilla, who had typed a short letter on stationery from the Hotel George V in Paris. I'm quite pretty, she wrote, and bright, and great in bed.

I should have told myself it didn't matter that Annette didn't have a car, or breasts, and I should have tossed Priscilla's's letter, and I should eat more green, leafy vegetables, but, really, who would lie about a thing like sex? I called Priscilla, and she asked me sooner than you might think whether I was handsome, and I said no, not especially, and she said, well, I don't suppose it matters. Come on over and bring a bottle of wine. And she thoughtfully told me exactly what wine to bring.

And greeted me at the door to her apartment in a white cotton nightgown. I would have said *mousy* before *quite pretty*, but either way, she took the wine in one hand, me in the other, and before you could say *French Colombard* we were sprawled on the couch with something by Mozart playing in the background. One of us— I think it may have been Priscilla—wrapped my fingers around her breasts. I suggested that we might be more comfortable in the bedroom, but that broke the mood, and as quickly as she'd beckoned, she backed away and began a rambling monologue about her painful search for a long-term relationship. I listened and nodded for awhile, apologized for having to leave so soon after my arrival, and wondered, as I walked back to my car, if her boyfriend had been watching from a closet.

OM NAMAH SHIVAYA

When one of my droll quips doubled her over with laughter on the steps of the Opera House, I was fairly certain, despite my limited experience, that Claire and I would become lovers. But I would not have imagined that she had dropped acid before she attended a performance of *Das Rheingold*, that she had a photograph of Gurumayi Chidvilasananda on her dresser, or that she got speeding tickets as often as haircuts. But that's one of the joys of falling in love—discovering what else you've fallen into.

I met Claire, like Marie, through work, but they had nothing else in common. Claire was as tall as I, with a regal bearing. She worked in commercial real estate and dressed accordingly—stylish suits and dresses, makeup verging on the theatrical, and nails that gleamed like a showroom Buick.

I didn't own a suit. I didn't like opera. I'd never chanted *om namah shivaya* at the Siddha Yoga Ashram kitty-corner from the Black Muslim Bakery in West Oakland. But I was a backpacker, so I was pleasantly surprised when Claire invited me to join her and a few of her friends on a weekend backpack trip in the Sierra foothills. She was happy to sleep on hard ground, but I was surprised to find her sitting on a log the next morning, applying mascara. That afternoon, the lot of us gamboled naked in warm sunshine, smoking dope and scrambling over granite outcroppings like monkeys at an Asian temple.

A couple of these friends invited Claire and me on a weeklong High Sierra backpack trip in August. After hauling a prodigious amount of food over steep terrain for three days, we set up camp and relaxed. Claire's friends, Stu and Audrey, dropped acid on a sunny morning, and Claire would normally have joined them, but because I was a rookie consumer of hallucinogenic substances, she'd brought magic mushrooms instead. We chewed them thoroughly, and I was soon gazing in wonder at majestic Banner Peak, whose geologic structure, indiscernible an hour before, now presented itself with sparkling clarity. Claire gave me a gentle poke. Let's talk about *us*, she said. I sensed trouble. I'd read somewhere that compromise is fundamental to any relationship, but why did she want to talk about *us* just as Banner Peak and I were becoming friends for life? Why not talk about *us* after dinner, or tomorrow, or in the car on the way home? Surely my many short-comings, which triggered her penchant for analysis, would still be there after the sky stopped buzzing. But the same could be said for Banner Peak, so we talked.

Mascara in the mountains proved to be an omen. I was dating a woman who would stop at three markets on a Friday afternoon to buy ingredients for a new recipe; chop, sauté and blend for an hour; plop a slice of lemon into each water glass on the dining room table; pause briefly to eat, and then immediately carry everything back to the kitchen, load the dishwasher, sponge the countertops, sweep the floor, go to bed, fall asleep five minutes after making love, and rise exuberantly the next morning in time to make an eight o'clock manicure. I, on the other hand, liked to sleep in while my dirty dishes ripened in the sink.

Claire didn't carry chains when we headed up to Squaw Valley to ski for the weekend. *What if it snows,* I'd ask? *Then we'll have an adventure,* she'd say. She took me to opening night at the opera, and I fell asleep twice. She organized a surprise birthday party at a toney French restaurant where then-Mayor Dianne Feinstein and her husband were dining two tables over. She sent me cards twice a week telling me that she loved me, but I didn't want to be loved so lavishly.

Claire's heart was as open as a barn door while mine was barely ajar. After the novel intertwining of our very different lives wasn't novel anymore, the one thing we continued to share was affection. Each of us took something from our time together. I felt love from someone who smiled with her whole being, and Claire came to appreciate whimsy. She'd been sent many bouquets in her time, but she'd never come home from work to find Raggedy Ann and Raggedy Andy sitting on a cookie sheet, rowing across her bed with wooden spoons.

(The Sounds of Silence)

I've lived alone all my adult life. My unspectacular procession of days moves through bands of light and shadow—restlessness, engrossment, anger, amusement, sorrow, and even contentment. Neither my heart nor my body has joined with a woman's for so long now that I'm like a car set on blocks in a weedy yard, the odds of ever running again slowly waning until at some point the moving parts have seized up beyond redemption. If I were honest, I would say that point has been reached, but it's easier to live without companionship if I believe that solitude is mine by choice.

I like women, and I respect them, and then I see an attractive woman half my age walking down the street and I resent her for being alluring and unobtainable. Or I meet a woman and think, *Now she would be a good companion* even as I know that two days of anyone's companionship will make me anxious to be stretched out alone on my couch with a book.

I know a few people who *found the right person* and seem truly content in their marriages and relationships. I used to wonder if there could have been a *right person* so right that she would have inspired even me to learn the skills of community. I wondered about mischievous Pauline, or about Alicia, a radiantly kind woman who once lived in my mother's downstairs apartment. My mother tried to play matchmaker in the most artless way possible, and she was right to try, but Alicia and I lived three hundred miles apart, and that let me off the hook. Finally, I wondered about a lovely young woman named Sarah. I wondered for years if she would have been flattered or perplexed or disheartened if she knew how much I wanted to get to know her and how afraid I was to try. I wonder if she would remember me at all.

I first saw Sarah at a dormitory dance early in my freshman year at Berkeley. Henry and I had gone hoping to meet someone, but I just leaned against the wall nervously smoking cigarettes. Henry approached two coeds standing together on the other side of the dance floor. He spoke to the one on the right, she shook her head and he turned and walked back. There it is, I thought. Henry asked and Henry was rejected. I thought the woman on the left resembled the actress Joanna Shimkus. How foolish it would have been even to consider asking her to dance.

I recognized Sarah immediately when I saw her more than a year later while the National Guard was stationed in Berkeley after the People's Park riots. Guardsmen had run a communication cable down

Dwight Way and several students were using it to jump rope. Sarah stood watching them with a grey kitten on her shoulder. Perfect, I thought. I'll approach her and ask what the kitten's name is. But my throat tightened immediately. *No. No, I can't.* I watched her briefly, then walked away with my stomach roiling.

And a year after that I was standing in line at Whelan's Smoke Shop. I turned around, and there she was in a yellow raincoat. She smiled at me. *Behind me*, I thought wildly, *She's smiling at someone behind me.* But she wasn't, and I seized up as if paralyzed. It was ludicrous and it was true. I didn't smile back. And then it was too late to smile back. Mortified, I turned away, paid for my cigarettes, and fled into the rain. This tiny incident provoked once again the endless, fruitless debate. *She was too pretty to be smiling at me. But she did smile at me. What's the worst thing that could have happened if I'd said something to her? She would have laughed in disbelief. Everyone would have laughed. Can't she see how shy I am?* I longed to be a monk in a mountain cave. I wondered if I would ever see her again, and I knew it wouldn't be any different if I did.

During my senior year, I registered for Urban Sociology, one of those vaguely defined courses that provided a forum for a white middle class professor to guilt-trip white middle class students for being white and middle class. The course had been assigned to one of the largest lecture halls on campus, but the number of registrants was greater than the number of seats, so they held a lottery. I came early and sat way up in the back. All the seats had been taken when I noticed Sarah standing at the front of the hall. I was astonished. Was it possible we'd be in the same class for a quarter? *Please, Lord, let both our names be called.* Mine soon was. I remained seated, listening and watching. She would react if she heard her name called, and if I saw her reaction, I'd know who she was. She glanced up, saw me watching and looked away. Several times. I was certain she recognized me. And then her name was called, too. I left the lecture hall and walked straight to the card file in Sproul Hall to look up Sarah Wyman. Her family lived in a small community down the Peninsula. She was a member of the Tri Delt sorority. I floated weightless for the rest of the afternoon.

I would arrive early for the Urban Sociology lecture each week and sit near the back, edgily keeping watch from behind a copy of *The Daily Californian*. Sarah would arrive with a friend, an older woman, and they would sit together. Sarah was stylish by Berkeley standards, often wearing a dress. She carried herself gracefully. She had soft eyes. I had no plan to introduce myself, to tell her I could picture her face and golden hair against that yellow raincoat. I wasn't going to trip theatrically and spill an armload of books onto her lap, but I couldn't take my eyes off her.

I began to sit in different places around the lecture hall, which meant that Sarah would sometimes be sitting behind me and I could focus on white guilt without distraction. One afternoon I sat in a short row down near the front. All the other seats in the row were empty. Sarah soon walked in, alone, through the side door to my left. I tensed. She walked up the nearest aisle, turned into my row and sat down next to me. Not two seats over. Next to me. I stared at my spiral-bound notebook and flushed a shade brighter than her rose-colored dress. Suddenly, I was out of excuses. She wouldn't scorn me if I spoke: *Where is your friend today? What do you think of the class so far?* Even better: *Hello. How are you?* with a sheepish grin to acknowledge the awkwardness I felt. But I said nothing, and as each moment passed it became more difficult to break the excruciating tension, easier to rationalize my silence. *It's too late now. It's much too late.* I was hugely relieved when the lecture began, but as I furtively watched her take notes in a pleasing hand, as I grimly took notes of my own, I knew

I would sit within touching distance, tortured and mute, until the hour was up and she closed her notebook and capped her pen and stood and walked away. I cried hard that night.

I didn't watch for her after that. I kept my head down and tried to be invisible until the quarter was over. But near the end of the year our eyes met briefly one more time as we walked toward each other on Telegraph Avenue. I thought I saw sadness in hers.

Tide Pool Healthcare
II. The Bunion

An oyster phoned his surgeon
In a state of great dismay;
I've got a nasty bunion
And it hasn't gone away.

It hurts to dance the minuet
It's difficult to ski.
It might be smart to operate
At once if you agree.

The surgeon sat behind her desk
And doodled on a pad.
She sketched a couple bunions
And she shaded them a tad.

She noted all the symptoms
She hypothesized a cure.
She thought she had an answer
But in truth she wasn't sure.

She strategized and agonized
And tried a different tack.

She finally found the answer
And she called the oyster back.

I'm not inclined to doubt you
And you've suffered heaven knows.
But how can you have a bunion
When you haven't any toes?

FAUX PAS

I'M BASICALLY ALLERGIC TO RESPONSIBILITY. I vote, I floss daily and I pay my bills on time, but I know my limits. I don't have houseplants or children, and I've never served time as a pet owner, never sifted through a litter box or purchased gluten-free dog food or had intimate conversations with a personal mammal, with one exception.

That would be Faux Pas. Faux Pas was a cat, although anyone fond of cats will understand that this is a little like saying LeBron James plays basketball or Emeril Lagasse likes to cook. I met Faux Pas when I moved into a spacious studio apartment beneath the house where she lived. She had been a close friend of the previous tenant, who was a Francophile, which will clarify how Faux Pas—who had six toes on each of her front paws—got her name. Not long after I moved in, my new landlord, Ruthanne, headed off to Provence for six months. She had a proposition for me. Take care of little Faupsie while I'm away, she said, and you can keep her if you like after I get back. Sort of a *lease/option to buy* arrangement to the extent that it makes a lick of sense to speak of owning a cat. Ownership notwithstanding, Faux Pas did become my roommate after Ruthanne returned from France.

It's not as though I'd never been around cats. My mother always had at least one while my sisters and I were growing up. Some were merely pleasant and durable, but others were spirited and feisty. I based my standards for the ideal cat on Corky, who my mother nursed with an eyedropper until he was weaned, and who was rumored to have been sired—mentored, certainly—by a bobcat. My forearms were often laced with his claw slashes and yet he could jump from the bed onto my mother's bare shoulders without leaving a mark. At breakfast, he would beg for a piece of cantaloupe rind, carry it outside, gorge on it and then throw up. Before dinner, he yowled at my mother until she gave him a slice of raw potato. Corky also had riskier tastes, and he learned to hop on three legs after a neighbor shot him for marauding his pigeons. A year or so later, Corky went missing. My mother called for him from the back porch for weeks, but we never saw him again. I suspect he went back for seconds.

At seven or eight pounds, Faux Pas was much smaller than Corky. She had the sort of gray fur often called blue, a dense, silky coat that paled to near white on her round and pliant tummy. While I had admired Corky's sledgehammer approach to life, I was equally taken by Faux Pas' sly sense of mischief and her devotion to ritual. She was always pleased when I arrived home from work because the first thing I did after I walked in the door was toss a fat handful of kibble into her tip-proof dish. She knew the sound of my old Porsche as it growled up the steep, narrow driveway to Ruthanne's house. When I stopped at the maibox, she would scamper down to meet me and begin a throaty monologue. And as I drove from the mailbox to the house, she'd race just in front of me, feigning terror.

On Saturdays, I walked down to get the mail and Faux Pas followed, stopping twenty or thirty feet short to sit and watch. Then, as I returned with urgent pleas for money from OxFam and Common Cause, she would tense up and eye me with the eyes of her saber-toothed ancestors until I broke into a sprint and chased her up the hill. "I'm going to get you, Faux Pas," I would say with dire menace, and she'd dash under the deck, give me a cool glance, and start washing her face.

There were only so many places in my apartment where—by some sequence of leaps and clambers and belly wriggles—a cat could go, and Faux Pas systematically found each one, determining whether it would serve best as a nap site or a surveillance point. Her first consideration was comfort. During the summer, she sprawled on the cool tile floor in the kitchen or in the shade on the deck. If it was raining when I left for work, she declined to go out and spent part of the day sleeping in a box of old clothing on an overhead shelf in a closet. I'd seen her open one of the folding closet doors by reaching under it with a paw, but I had no idea how she got up to the shelf until I saw her jump to the top of my guitar case, which stood leaning into a corner, and then inch around to jump again.

When it was cold, Faux Pas slept in front of the wall heater, or, if I was writing at my desk, she might curl up under my goose-necked lamp. She usually slept with me at night, and I took this to be a social gesture, though by then I'd turned off the heater and the lamp. I sleep on my side, so she tucked herself into my knees or wedged up against my back. On one truly cold night she crawled under the covers, but she didn't stay long, perhaps thinking, as I sometimes did, that I ought to change the sheets more often.

Like all cats, Faux Pas slept a lot. When she was awake, she attended to personal hygiene, usually her own, although occasionally she licked my forehead or the back of my hand. I liked to watch her groom, addressing all that gray fur with her pink tongue until she met her standard of cleanliness or got bored or ran out of spit. Sometimes I helped her. She'd be stretched out on her side, laundering her flank one lick after another, and I'd hunker down next to her and tap her thigh. "You missed a spot," I'd say. "See? Right here." She'd stop licking, arch back like a cobra and regard me as if I'd passed wind in church. Then she'd resume laundering and I'd let her get in a few licks before I tapped her again or tugged gently on one of her hind legs. Faux Pas limited herself to two or three baleful glares before she went *sanpaku* and counterattacked. Then it became a contest to see who had the faster reflexes, and sooner or later she literally nailed me.

Although sleeping and bathing kept her busy, Faux Pas was willing to eat as often as I fed her, which, apart from the odd treat, was twice a day. She purred like a generator while she ate, oblivious to the rest of the universe, and I exploited her bliss to comb her for fleas. In warm weather there could be a lot of them even though I combed her daily. I hoped they weren't tormenting her, but to find five or ten of them after a few pulls was satisfying work, like hauling in a net heavy with fish. I became skilled, running the comb deep enough to snare the vermin at skin level but not combing too hard, and easing up when I came to a tangle of fur so Faups wouldn't swat me.

Faux Pas could be affectionate, but she picked her

moments, which is one of many things that cats have over dogs. If she leaned into my leg or settled on my lap, I felt that her spare affection had been earned. But if a dog—barely able to hold its course on account of its frantically whipping tail—raced up to plant muddy paws on my pants or drip slobber on my shirt, I tried not to take it personally. Which may be how Faux Pas felt when I cradled her in my arms and nuzzled her nose to nose. She didn't much like it, but she grew tolerant over time, supposing that if I had real kids to cuddle, they'd chase her and pull her tail.

Faux Pas was not a voluble conversationalist, but we talked occasionally. None of that itty bitty catty watty chatter, but a mature exchange. "How was your day, Faux Pas? Did you have a good day?" Or, when she was moistening a paw to scrub one of her ears, "Are you being a cat? Are you busy being a cat?"

These conversations were usually one-sided. Sometimes she ignored me completely or merely looked at me with mild curiosity, but sometimes she responded. "Mrrrp?" she would say in a nasal tone. "Mrrrp?"

"That's right," I would answer.

"Mrrrp?"

"Right again."

"Mrrrp?"

"You tell 'em, Faups."

Faux Pas fancied herself a hunter. She stalked me from beneath my desk, vibrating in moon-eyed, pre-assault mode, springing forth to tackle my ankles and then veering off to careen around the room once or twice at full stretch. If she'd had just a bit more catpower, centrifugal force would have allowed her to sail around the walls like a cyclist in a velodrome.

She stalked smaller game outside, sometimes leaving feathers scattered on the deck to remind me that allowing her to roam freely was an indulgence with a cost. One night she sneaked a mouse into the apartment. When she began playing catch-and-release-and-catch-and-release, the mouse made straight for the crack under the front door, but, finding that it couldn't squeeze under, it crawled under the loose edge of the carpet instead. It was an admirable move and I decided to spare this mouse the horror of slow death by chewing, but each time I lifted the carpet to help it escape, the fright-addled creature wedged in further. Had I been Mother Teresa, I would have pulled the whole carpet up or called the fire department, but as it was I looked sorrowfully at the slight bulge beneath the Berber, put my full weight to it, pulled the flattened mouse out by the tail and tossed it off the deck.

Such was our quiet life together, and the two of us formed a multitude for several years. Then a workmate showed me the unit she'd bought in the only housing complex in the county where I could possibly afford to live. My mother helped with the down payment, and twenty years after college I was finally able to talk mortgage with my friends.

Faux Pas hid under the couch for two days after we moved, which surprised me because she'd always been fearless. She got her boat righted after a week or so, but she wouldn't go outside, and that surprised me, too. How did she plan to get her exercise? By raising hell inside instead of out, that's how, but with a crucial difference: she adjusted her schedule. Now, boxes mysteriously toppled from shelves at three o'clock in the morning. Or I would be awakened by the gentlest, most considerate tapping of a paw on my cheek. I endured these tortures for a few days. After all, moving is a stressful event for everyone concerned, and we'd moved for my benefit, not hers. But the disruption of my sleep soon became more than a simple annoyance, and I feared that, provoked to groggy rage, I might do my housemate serious harm. Reluctantly, I called Ruthanne, and she agreed to take Faux Pas back.

There were advantages to living cat-free. I didn't

have to daub my black clothes with wads of tape to remove discarded fur. Fleas didn't effervesce from the carpet when the weather got hot. And Faux Pas was only a twenty-minute drive away, although I didn't visit often. Then, tragedy struck. Ruthanne had installed an automatic garage door opener, and Faux Pas, who liked to clamber around up under the roof, got caught in the machinery. I was thankfully spared the details, but it was a fatal mishap. *You had a darn good life right up to the end, Faups,* I thought after I'd had a good cry. *I hope your next eight will be even better.*

Tide Pool Healthcare
III. The Headache

A starfish phoned her doctor
In the middle of the night.
I hope I didn't wake you, Doc
But here's my woeful plight.

I've got a splitting headache
So I called my Uncle Squid.
He tried to give me aspirin
But he jammed the squid-proof lid.

Her doctor rubbed his bleary eyes
And brewed a cup of tea.
He stirred a little sugar in
And then he said let's see.

He sought a diagnosis
From a dozen points of view.
I thought I'd seen it all he mused
But this is something new.

He nearly fell asleep and then
He had a brilliant notion.

He quickly called the starfish
At her home beside the ocean.

I know you're always honest
I don't question what you've said.
But how can you have a headache
When you haven't got a head?

THE COLLECTIONS

I'M NOT A HOARDER. I'M AN ARCHIVIST. If I were a hoarder and you opened the front door to my condo, you would encounter narrow paths leading to the kitchen and the bathroom between floor to ceiling stacks of old newspapers, greasy pizza boxes and back issues of *Arizona Highways*.

You won't see any of these in my condo, but here's a partial list of what you will see: nine glazed ceramic duck figurines (mostly mallard drakes); seven wall-mounted allegedly collectible plates featuring ducks serenely floating on ponds; seven framed illustrations of ducks taking flight; twelve framed handbills for '60s concerts at Winterland, Fillmore West and the Avalon Ballroom; a set of elk antlers; two kukui nut leis from my eldest grandnephew's first birthday celebration in Hawaii; a suspended, internally illuminated *Bud Lite* point of purchase display; a framed portrait of Paris Hilton; a Sergeant Pepper cookie jar; a solar-powered mariachi band; and a bona fide Soviet army fur hat for those chilly nights on the steppes. Oh, and about 3,500 neatly shelved record albums, but more on that later.

About the ducks: For my money, the mallard drake was the icon sine qua non of the Midwest culture of the

'50s that kids like me who lived on the West Coast never knew except in our Dick and Jane readers. But if you grew up in, say, Iowa, you raked leaves every autumn and constructed snowmen every winter while your uncle and a couple of his buddies froze their asses off hunkered down in a blind somewhere outside of town waiting for a squadron of quacking mallards to fly overhead.

Easter Eggs

If you drive around the residential neighborhoods in the hillier parts of Seattle, you'll see a fair number of rockeries on the sloped ground between the houses and the streets below. Often, there are clusters of small flowers poking up between the dark, angular rocks. Our front lawn was flat, so the rockeries that ran down either side of it weren't necessary, but they were a friendly tip of the hat to their cousins on the hill behind us, and they too were sprinkled with flowers.

I was four or five years old when Kath and I participated in our first Easter egg hunt. Our mother would have bought a PAAS egg decorating kit at Thriftway so that Judy could dye a dozen or so eggs in pleasing pastel colors. Then, presumably after Kath and I were asleep on Easter Eve, the two of them hid the eggs in the rockeries, so that they became spots of color among the flowers. Some subtlety was required here. If the placement of the eggs was too obvious, they'd be snatched up in a few minutes, and where's the fun in that? Conversely, if they were hidden like Japanese snipers on Tarawa, we would never find them on our own, which, in my case, would probably have led to tears of frustration, followed by an adult pointing and saying, *Look, Stanton, what's that next to the yellow flower? No, no, on the other side of the yellow flower.* In brief, a loving but critical assessment of my core competency.

Things often seem happier in retrospect. What I remember now is The Hunt. My pleasure came not from finding but from looking. After all, what self-respecting five-year-old wants a hardboiled egg? You could peel it and push your finger against the rubbery white part, but then what? In a few months, you'd come home from an evening of trick-or-treating with much more seductive swag. No, it was the looking, and it's been the looking ever since. Every time I go to Goodwill or the Salvation Army or a garage sale or an estate sale, I'm a five-year-old looking for Easter eggs. Often, I don't find anything, but I still got to look, although I'd be the first to acknowledge that I don't need another record album or

CD or DVD. Or another Jerry Garcia necktie to go with the nearly 300 I already have. Of course, if I do find one I have to buy it. Because that's what archivists do.

Pebbles

The acorn didn't make it far from the tree. My mother, wearing pants worn through from rubbing, once scoured the ocean beaches north of Arcata looking for pieces of jade. She brought likely suspects home, separated the keepers from the also-rans, added the former to her growing collection and discarded the rest. Clad in equally worn Levis, I drive out to the Marin coast once a week or so to scrutinize patches of gravel along the beaches. There's no jade to be found, but there are a variety of attractive pebbles, and I usually drop a fat handful or two into a Ziploc bag to take home for thorough assessment.

My criteria for a potentially collectible pebble are symmetry, smoothness, translucency, uniform color, and shininess. These criteria eliminate 99.99% of the pebbles on the beach, ensuring a challenging search, and, more to the point, keeping the size of my collection manageable. The translucent pebbles range from milky white through yellow and amber to a beautifully rich orange-red. Many are no bigger than a pea. I display these pebbles in a clear glass dish on the coffee table and insist that guests ooh and aah when I backlight them with a flashlight.

I rarely see other beachcombers, in part because the National Park Service has reflexively imposed its *Take only photos, Leave only footprints* dictum, but also because you have to get down on your hands and knees to find the little buggers. And even then they're easy to miss, especially if they've been dulled by a scum of salt. In that case, the trick is to lick off the salt and then rub the pebble against your pant leg to bring up the sheen. Note to the NPS: I periodically take my also-rans back to the beach and dump them in the surf.

I look for smooth stones whenever the opportunity presents itself. On several canoe trips in Canada's Mackenzie Mountains, I wandered along the shore after dinner looking for appealing cobbles of granite. They were almost always too heavy to haul back to civilization, so I piled them up in interesting ways, or photographed them in situ, or both. When I accompanied Kath and my brother-in-law on a trip to Campobello, they headed out to visit local features of historic interest, and I asked to be dropped off at the beach where Eleanor Roosevelt once collected round stones. These were only an inch or two in diameter, so I brought home a dozen in a wonderfully delicate range of colors—pinkish brown, light grey, grey-green and buff. I assume Eleanor will one day communicate with me through our respective collections, but nothing so far, at least that I can detect.

Years ago, I was headed out on a solo backpacking trip south of Yosemite when I was struck on the thigh by a small bouncing boulder that knocked me ass over tea kettle off the trail. I only got a quick glance at the boulder, which looked to be a bit smaller than a cantaloupe. When I got home, I realized that I had a similar boulder—a real beauty—displayed in my living room. I had misappropriated it from Illilouette Creek, which is in Yosemite, which is a National Park. Probably just a coincidence.

NECKWEAR

Disclosure: I am not a Deadhead. I concede that the band came up with a few snappy tunes over the decades— "Sugar Magnolia" comes to mind—but to my ear Jerry Garcia was an often undisciplined guitarist whose noodlings would have been best suited to the soundtrack for *A Voyage to Neptune*. And let's be honest here, the Dead didn't sing all that well.

On the other hand, Jerry briefly attended the San Francisco Art Institute before he became known as a musician, and the man had talent as a painter. In time, his artwork became the inspiration for J. Garcia neckties, which are still sold in an apparently never-ending succession of wild patterns and colors. I collect J. Garcia ties because I like those wild patterns and colors, and, to paraphrase the would-be Mount Everest summiteer George Mallory, *because they're there. There* in this case usually being the Goodwill store on Third Street.

I suspect that most J. Garcia ties are purchased as gifts for men who either don't wear ties—and these days that's most of us—or who prefer ties that are less exuberant, and that's most of us, too. But you don't have to wear them to admire their woozy vibrancy. For example, I've used them to form valances for the windows in my living room and bedrooms. I folded them twice and hung them from rows of clothes pins secured above the windows with double-stick tape. The ties overlap sideways like anorexic shingles to create a mass of busy color. First time visitors are rightfully impressed.

In addition to the J. Garcia ties, I have a bunch of antique ties from the '40s and '50s, and a dozen skinny, square-bottomed Ernst ties, which architects during the '60s were required to wear along with their blue work shirts, baggy wide wale corduroy pants, and Earth Shoes. I have Armani ties and Beatles ties and a Magic

Johnson and two Versaces, which are remarkably unattractive when you consider what the original owners must have paid for them. I have a yellow Smiley Face tie, several Mickey Mouse ties, an I Love Jesus tie, a Dilbert Christmas tie, a Viagra tie, and—are you sitting down?—two Rush Limbaugh ties, which are DayGlo bright and wilder than anything else in my collection.

JUST FOR THE RECORDS

I have, finally, a collection of record albums, or, as they are collectively known, vinyl. There are about 3,500 of them, which is a lot by almost anyone's standards. Stacked like pancakes, they'd form a wobbly tower five stories high. Laid out end to end, they'd extend well more than half a mile. But everything is relative. My friend and trading partner Mickey has about 15,000 albums, and the owner of Village Music, a long-gone but still legendary Mill Valley record store, is said to have three or four times that.

I keep my albums in a dozen modular shelving units designed specifically for this purpose. The units are all virtually full, so when a record comes in the door—which doesn't happen all that often these days—another one goes out. The keepers are stored alphabetically by genre, including Classical Music, Rock'n'Roll, Pop,

Soul, Folk, Country, Musicals, Soundtracks, Bachelor Pad Music, Comedy and Spoken Word. More obscure categories include *Learn to Speak* records for Arabic, Serbo-Croatian, Finnish et al, and collections of polite cover versions of rock'n'roll hits for listeners who don't like rock'n'roll. "Light My Fire" by the Lettermen, for example, or "Black Magic Woman" by Percy Faith & His Orchestra.

To qualify as a keeper, a record must meet at least one of the following criteria: 1) I like the music; 2) I like the cover art; 3) It's in really good shape; 4) It has significant value, and/or 5) It doesn't necessarily meet any of these requirements, but it's really wacky. Good examples here would be *Peter and the Wolf* narrated by William F. Buckley, Jr. and *Dr. Dante's Neurothaianetic Figure Control Record for Women*.

Where did all these records come from? From thrift stores and estate sales, certainly, and from trading with used record stores and other collectors. But mostly from hundreds and hundreds of Saturday morning garage sales. In the day, I got organized after work on Friday evening, scanning the garage sale section in the *Marin Independent Journal* classified ads and crossing out the ones that led off with outgrown baby clothes or used NordicTracks. I chose fifteen or twenty addresses within reasonable driving distance, checked my maps to locate unfamiliar streets, and made notes like *Sir Francis Dr 1st right after Butterfield, left Suffield*. Then I ranked the addresses in an efficient driving sequence and put my notes, maps and a couple bagels next to the front door. 7:00am on a Saturday morning is not a good time to be thinking about logistics.

I was not alone as I drove from garage to garage. For every seller hoping to trade clutter for cash, there were dozens of potential buyers eager to reciprocate, and among them were other record collectors with notes and maps and alarm clocks of their own. I hoped for the same scenario they did, that I would pull up to the curb a full hour before the published opening time to find the homeowners just beginning to lug their wares out to the driveway. *My, you're up early*, they would say, not with irritation but to acknowledge my dedication. I'd respond with casual good humor as I eyed their chipped Crock-Pots and old sweatshirts and stacks of romance novels, ready to close in on the Search Object like a stooping hawk. But where is the cardboard box full of pristine albums? I sidle closer. *Will you be selling any records today?* They will. *Hon, this man wants to look at the records*. I graciously offer to help lug the heavy box out from the garage.

It did happen like this more than once, but if I showed up at 7:00am I'd be much more likely to find the garage door closed. Or to be shooed away, sometimes not politely. And when I came back at 9:00am, the box of records, if there was one, would be half empty—evidence, probably, that at least one other collector had already gone through it. What was left would be the likes of Herb Albert and the Tijuana Brass. No surprise there. The record bins in every thrift store known to man have at least one of his albums tucked in among *John Denver's Greatest Hits, 101 Strings Play Broadway Favorites, The Great Songs of Christmas Volume 5* and a snoozer or two by Andy Williams. Imagine flipping through a bin of CDs and finding nothing but Enya and Ottmar Liebert.

As time went on, people were less willing to part with their records. *We're keeping ours*, they'd say emphatically, as if I were trying to hoodwink them out of their life savings. And certainly some albums were worth hanging onto—old jazz and R&B, Bachelor Pad Music, or vintage rock from the '60s. But condition is a factor often overlooked. Most of the rock albums of the '60s, for example, were stacked three or four deep on record changers to grind against each other like millstones. They were handled with gooey fingers, played with

281

worn needles, anointed with spilled wine and then aged for years in dank basements. No one wants them now. That's why they go to thrift stores and never leave.

On the other hand, suppose you find a copy of *In-A-Gadda-Da-Vida*, not the reissue with the yellow label, but the original pressing with the purple and brown label. Suppose further that the prior owner never listened to this record while he was so ripped that he could barely open a package of Oreos, never mind keep his sugary thumbprints to himself. Congratulations! You've just found a Near Mint copy. Look it up in the *Goldmine Record Album Price Guide* and you'll find a listed value of $25.00. Lives there a soul who would pay it? Maybe, if you could find him, but it would be a whole lot easier to go to a used record store, where you might get three or four dollars in trade. Or you might not. *Goldmine* lists a Near Mint mono copy of the Baysiders' *Over the Rainbow* at $200.00. *Terrific,* I thought when I found a clean copy. *This will be good for thirty bucks in trade.* Wrong. The two used record stores I took it to weren't interested at any price. *Can't sell it,* they said.

If the collector's guides were giddily optimistic about what my records were worth, it's also true that I'd paid little enough to acquire them, fifty cents or a dollar in nearly every case. Had I paid myself minimum wage and thrown in the cost of gas, it would have been five times that, but how crass to put a price on the thrill of the chase, the irritation at yet another sale with more signs than merchandise, or the dismay at finding a Jimmy Hendrix album that had apparently been used as a chew toy by a Rottweiler. Record collecting is like sex: block out most of your time for anticipation.

At the end of a Saturday morning I might have had five records or fifty. Either way, like an archeologist slapping the dust off her pants after the day's last clamber from a dig, I wasn't finished until I'd examined my treasures and restored them. I used paper towels and Windex to clean the dust and smudges off the covers, lighter fluid to remove price stickers, and discreet lengths of Magic Mending Tape to close up split edges. I gently scrubbed dirty records with a cleaning solution and then spun them on my Nitty Gritty, a sort of specialized vacuum cleaner that sucked up dust motes and fingerprints. I put the records inside their covers and the covers inside clear plastic sleeves. Then I began fantasizing about what I might find the following Saturday.

For many years, there were two albums I coveted but had never seen anywhere, in any condition, at any price. I could have gone online, but that would have been cheating. I finally got copies of both of them in unexpected ways.

The Shadows Know!!! by The Shadows: I was sitting in a meeting with a wonderfully wacky client—an interior architect named Clara—and I noticed that she was taking notes with a fountain pen and brown ink. After the meeting, I complimented her on her unconventional choice of a writing implement. "Oh, Thomas and I collect fountain pens," she said with considerable animation. "We go to fountain pen conventions!" Now, as it happened, I had several antique fountain pens that once belonged to Grandma Klose. They were attractive to me in their antiquity, but they sat in a drawer unvisited unless I opened it looking for something else. So I brought the pens to my next meeting with Clara and asked her if she would like to have them. She nearly swooned.

"Are you sure?" she gasped. I said yes. So she asked what she could give me in return, and I said, well, there's an album by a British band called...Several days later, a record-sized package addressed to me arrived at the office. *The Shadows Know!!!* was in funky shape, but it hardly mattered.

Sylvie À Nashville by Sylvie Vartan: Sylvie was a svelte come-hitherish French pop singer from the '60s who sang in both French and English. (Actually, as I learned years later, her mother was Hungarian, her father was half Bulgarian and half Armenian, and

Vartan was originally Vartanian: The family had moved to France as refugees from Communism.) Anyway, one of my college roommates had a copy of the album, and, on first hearing, I wanted one too. I never imagined I would stumble onto this album at a garage sale, but when I began poking around in used record stores, I always checked the French Vocalists section. I eventually found several of Sylvie's albums, but not the one I really wanted. Then, providentially, I had some friends over for dinner, and one of them mentioned a painting I had done many years before. She'd always liked it, and it had been hibernating in my closet for decades, so I asked her if she would like to have it. "Oh, no," she said. "I couldn't possibly take it." So I proposed a trade. I would give her the painting if she would track down Sylvie. She wasn't able to find the record, but she did find a CD which included not just the original twelve tracks but sixteen bonus tracks to boot. A fair trade, I thought.

Bud & Connie

Prologue

In 1941, newlyweds Harmon and Constance Helmericks
traveled by canoe into northern Alaska, where they
built a cabin, overwintered, and lived off the land.
They wrote several books about this and other
adventures, and I have them all.

Bud and Connie paddled north on flowing water
Bud set course while Connie clubbed a river otter.

Bud and Connie shot a bear beside the river
Bud and Connie skinned it there and ate the liver.

Bud and Connie built a home from hand-cut stacks of
Lincoln Logs that Bud and Connie chinked the cracks of.

Bud and Connie trapped for rabbits in the fall
Connie snapped their furry necks and fried them all.

Bud said, Connie, rabbit meat will never do
We must go after bigger game; a moose or two.

Consequently Bud went hunting in the woods
And soon a single moose-bound bullet dropped the goods.

Connie's moose drew seven shots in quick succession
Six went wide. The seventh made a big impression.

Bud pursued a wolverine upwind. Its
Eyes were red. Bud shot it dead and skinned it.

Bud and Connie stalked a herd of caribou
Connie eyed the plumpest three and shot them, too.

Many creatures roamed the land;
Our heroes saw a host of them.
They kept their rifles close at hand
and put a hole in most of them.

ICEBERGS

I WAS OUT ON THE LAND AFTER DINNER, wandering near our campsite over stone-cobbled hills, when I looked up to see an Arctic fox loping toward me about twenty yards off. The fox seemed as surprised as I. It slowed, stopped and regarded me as I spoke in reassuring tones. *Hey, fox,* I said. *What's up?* The fox held my gaze for a couple of beats and then angled past me and disappeared over a rise as I admired its fluid gait. This was the first time I'd seen an Arctic fox, and likely the first time it had encountered a human being. We met around eleven on a sunny evening on Canada's Ellesmere Island, which is west of northern Greenland and, where we were, maybe 700 miles from the North Pole. Foxes live on Ellesmere because they can tolerate minus forty-degree weather and dine on bird eggs and lemmings and the table scraps of polar bears. Tourists—a very few of us—come to visit in July and August because the temperature then is often fifty or sixty degrees above zero, and because, being in some respects more clever than foxes, we can bring with us whatever foods we like.

I had come to Ellesmere, as I had to other places in the High Arctic, in part to see the animals. Walruses and seals in the fiords; Arctic foxes, Arctic hares and an occasional muskox ashore; Arctic terns overhead. But in a way the Arctic appeals to me less for what it offers than for what it lacks. I believe that we humans who live in a world comprised mainly of human artifacts cannot feel truly at home while our ancestors continue to speak to us through our genes about the many thousands of years when human awareness was framed essentially by land and sky. I can point to little in present-day culture to support this contention—except, perhaps, the remarkable extent to which images of the natural world appear in ads for SUVs that never leave paved roads—but our collective noise and constant motion can be wearying. The Arctic is an unusually quiet place where I can try to imagine what it would have been like to live before technology, before cities, before language. I know what we've gained from these things. I wonder what we've lost. I wonder about the texture and spark of Paleolithic consciousness.

I first saw wilderness worthy of the name when my friend, Dave, invited me to join him and his friend, Jim, on a backpacking trip out of Yosemite Valley. Dave's plan was for us to hike up the Merced River Canyon to Merced Lake and back during the last week of October. The weather was gloomy when we arrived in Yosemite late on a Saturday afternoon, and we were surprised, though we shouldn't have been, when rain began drumming on our tent in the middle of the night. It was still raining the next morning, so we packed up, drove home, and returned a week later to set out at the beginning of November, the latest I've ever been in the High Sierra.

I improvised on equipment. Kath loaned me the tired orange backpack she'd bought at a thrift shop, and I filled it with warm clothes, my new down sleeping bag, a cheap plastic poncho, my share of the freeze-dried food, three packs of cigarettes and a five cell flashlight for the long nights. The flashlight alone weighed several pounds. I wondered, as I struggled to shoulder the pack, whether I could make it to the trailhead on the other side of the parking lot.

The hike up out of Yosemite Valley is not an after dinner stroll. The trail, which climbs about three thousand feet in the first few miles, is for many stretches a steep rock staircase. I started out too fast and spent as much time slumped on boulders gasping for breath as I did walking. Sweat lubricated my nose so that my glasses slid down as many times as I pushed them back up. My poorly adjusted shoulder straps made my arms go numb. When I finally arrived at our campsite, the tent was up and dinner was almost ready.

The trail rose more gently the next day, paralleling

the river and sometimes crossing its course over broad granite slabs. I began to notice the huge boulders, the steely cloud cover and the chill wind at our backs. The wind put us on notice that we were venturing into the mountains at the edge of winter, and each gust set off shivers of wariness and excitement. We passed occasional backpackers coming down from the high country with a week's worth of stubble on their chins and ice axes strapped to their packs. Even as my shoulders ached and blisters formed on my feet, I wondered where they had been and what they had seen.

We camped for two days in a sun-starved canyon seventeen miles in. The ground was wet from melting snow. The open country to the east was too far to reach on a day hike, and the granite mountainsides that surrounded us were too steep to clamber up. We raided a nearby horse camp for firewood, but it was still too cold to stay outdoors much after dark, especially now that our boots were wet. So we spent the long nights in the tent, where we might have used my flashlight to read or play Hearts if one of us had thought to bring a book or a deck of cards. Instead, we listened uneasily to the weird shrieks of squabbling coyotes. We hiked the seventeen miles back to the car in one day and then drove home. The next morning, I crawled out of bed on my hands and knees.

I might have concluded that backpacking is a cumbersome form of masochism, and it still feels that way on the first day of every trip I take. But Dave and I did a less exhausting trip the next summer, and I began to do two or three trips almost every summer after that, sometimes with friends, sometimes alone. I explored and I learned. I soon found that I preferred high exposed terrain where the vistas of peaks and ridges were uninterrupted by trees, and the warming sun rose early on frosty mornings. Some of my early backpacking companions measured our success by the number of miles we'd covered, and I'll admit that I enjoyed seeing disbelief on the faces of the freshly-scrubbed day hikers who asked us—grimy and disheveled after a week on the trail—where we'd been and how far we've come. But my goal was soon clear: to haul my pack only as long as necessary to reach an alpine meadow which would serve as a base camp for two or three days of hiking.

Many backpackers are pilgrims of a sort who walk the same worn trails to reach the same spectacular destinations and claim the same trampled campsites. But because I value solitude more than spectacle, I began to explore less popular areas that had all the wonder, if not the scale—and the marauding bears—of Yosemite. When I became comfortable leaving a trail and setting out cross-country, I was able to spend days in silence if I chose to, and by this time I was often traveling alone. My erstwhile backpacking partners had gained twenty pounds or become parents or concluded that the rewards no longer matched the effort. I much preferred company in the mountains—a companion or two with whom I could share a sky filled with stars or a bar of chocolate, but I also had moments of exultation and deep satisfaction as I moved on my own along a route of my choosing.

It took years and many trips to learn how to maximize my comfort and safety in the mountains. To use moleskin to prevent blisters rather than to lessen their pain. To keep an eye on the morning sky and re-consider a long ridge walk if the clouds foretold a thunderstorm. But a fundamental truth was unavoidable: that despite everything I've learned, the first day on the trail— trudging up one switchback after another, sucking in the lean air at eight or nine or ten thousand feet above sea level, lurching beneath a week's worth of food—would seem to take forever and end in dull exhaustion. And (at least in retrospect) be worth it. Worth it to reaffirm that life need not be lived solely indoors, that a landscape can be much more than scenery glimpsed through a windshield. Worth it because the sky at ten thousand feet is so thick with blue and the granite peaks against it are so sharp and bright that the jagged line between them nearly sizzles. Because I can walk around a mountain lake and attain my goal with each step. And by the third or fourth day, my lungs will have adjusted to the altitude so that I can scamper up the last thirty feet to a mountain crest to confirm that there are, in fact, more mountains on the other side. I've reached a satisfying mastery I may never know as fully in any other part of my life.

My mother was a native Finn, and after several summers in the mountains, I traded a season of backpacking to join her and Kath on a three-week visit to the land of her birth. She had been back several times to visit relatives, but this was my first trip, and it was surprisingly emotional. A United Airlines TV commercial at the time featured a young Japanese American who was flying to his parents' homeland, *returning for the first time*. That was how I felt, that my Finnish heritage had so shaped me that Finland seemed familiar as soon as we stepped off the plane.

The day we arrived, one of my second cousins took us on an evening tour of Helsinki. It was July, and still light at eleven o'clock. At one point, we stood on a promontory above the Wärtsilä Shipyard, where huge icebreakers were at rest in the harbor, and nearby streets were almost empty of people and traffic. The whole panorama glowed in butter-yellow light. I was mesmerized.

My mother, Kath and I spent a week in Helsinki and then set off east and north. The Finnish countryside was nearly flat by California standards, but the forests and glacial undulations gave it cozy scale, and there were so many lakes and peninsulas and islands that it seemed we were always looking across water to a nearby shore. We stayed with relatives at their lakeside summer cottages, walking through the woods, rowing between islands, and baking in their saunas. The knock and creak of oars in their oarlocks drew me back to my childhood, to our lakefront home in Seattle and to Pear Point, where the rocky shoreline and the brambles and mosses were uncannily similar. I teared up with nostalgia.

The three of us sat one evening on a park bench in the small city of Jyväskylä. There was a drunk nearby—this was, after all, Scandinavia—and a group of punkish teenagers were rehearsing menace, but we were pretty sure the alertness that would be instinctive in many American cities was unnecessary here. The evening was warm and serene, and the serenity seemed linked to the light, the same benevolent light we'd seen in Helsinki.

I remembered that light long after my sadness at leaving Finland had dissipated, after I'd stopped yearning to move there and spend my summers rowing across its lakes.

Two years after the Finnish pilgrimage, I paid a deposit to reserve my place on a three-week trek to the base camp of Mt. Everest. I was now a dues paying admirer of mountains, and here was an opportunity to see the tallest one of all, a mountain twice as high as any in California. And not just to see it, but to approach it, stride by stride, day after day, until my trekking companions and I stood nine miles from the summit. It was a journey of 180 miles at altitudes as high as 18,000 feet.

I was apprehensive about travel to a third world country, but the government of Nepal welcomed tourism as an important source of foreign exchange and tried to maintain a benign environment for visitors. And once on the trail, our guide would watch to see that his clients didn't get themselves into serious trouble. We were pampered. The porters would bring us bowls of hot water at first light, then strike the tents and carry our duffle bags to the next campsite. The kitchen staff would set out early to have lunch ready at midday. All we had to do was tie our shoelaces and hike eight or ten miles a day on steep terrain. I relished the immediacy of life on the trail. I was so far from home and so unreachable that I could spend one day and then another just moving and looking, never wondering whether I'd remembered to pay my phone bill.

For the first week or so, we hiked generally east, up and down wooded ridges along the base of the Himalayan spine, through villages without power or running water. I saw the deforestation and erosion that overpopulation had caused, and I saw villagers with amoebic dysentery cough up grotesque streams of mucus. I also saw elegantly built stone houses set among neatly tended fields below white peaks and clear skies.

The scale of the mountains and canyons was hard to discern, but they were enormous, especially after we turned north and began ascending the Khumbu Valley below Everest. We entered a great, empty amphitheater carpeted in dull stone and enclosed by ice-fluted peaks of impossible steepness. The sky was dark blue, close to indigo. It was cold. Cold in the daytime and colder at night, and I hadn't brought enough insulation for either. Each night I huddled in my sleeping bag until my bladder compelled me to dash out of the tent beneath stars that dazzled in the thin atmosphere.

My trekking companions and I slogged and panted, finally, to Kala Patthar, an overlook 500 feet above

Everest Base Camp. We sat for half an hour photographing a dark, broad peak that, from our vantage point, looked underdressed for its role as the highest point on the planet. Then we headed back down the trail for four more days and flew from the airstrip at Lukla to Kathmandu, where the temperature was seventy-five degrees and our hotel had plenty of hot water.

I thought well enough of my time in Nepal to study Nepalese so I could speak a little of the language when I went back, but I haven't returned. I've wondered what it would be like to revisit the Himalayas with a middle-aged perspective and a warmer sleeping bag, but there were too many trekkers then and probably too many now, even after years of war and the recent catastrophic earthquake. Once was enough.

I continued to backpack in the High Sierra after my journeys to Finland and Nepal, but I'd developed a tickling curiosity about the Far North. I began to read books by adventurous married couples who built log cabins in northern wilderness and wintered over in northern darkness with frost forming on nail heads a few feet from the stove. I wanted to see this country, and, as an American, I might well have gone first to Alaska, but I had read Bob Marshall's *Alaska Wilderness,* and I was pretty sure I couldn't match his tolerance for wet weather, tortuous hiking conditions and hordes of single-minded mosquitoes. I was, however, intrigued by an ad I saw for a wilderness travel company in Vancouver, BC. I wrote for their brochure—I have since spent many hours poring over similar brochures, rereading the upbeat sales pitches for trips to all sorts of northern backwaters—and found that they led canoe trips down mountain rivers in Canada's Yukon Territory. I'd only been in a canoe once, and helped capsize it in a foot of water, but I signed up for one of their trips anyway. Two weeks in a vast roadless tract sprinkled with caribou and moose and grizzlies. Oh, my.

We—ten people and five canoes—were ferried in a single-engine floatplane to our put-in point, a small lake at the headwaters of the Wind River. I buckled into the co-pilot's seat and watched intently for two hours as we flew not much faster than freeway speed and no higher than necessary over a series of drainages until the pilot banked down to the lake. The next day, we portaged the canoes and our gear half a mile, then reloaded the canoes and lined them for several more miles until the river was deep enough for paddling.

The Wind was a Skill Level 1 river with nothing more challenging than the odd riffle—a good match to my lack of experience. I would paddle in the bow with one of the guides in the stern. I wasn't expected to navigate, only to respond to occasional commands to draw or cross draw or back paddle, so I was free to daydream within reason. I thought about the relative merits of canoeing and backpacking, and concluded that canoeing has two advantages. First, rivers flow downhill, so unless you're dealing with a murderous headwind, you'll be making progress even if you never put your paddle in the water. Second, paddling or not, you get to sit down. Conversely, there are two principal disadvantages to canoeing, at least as I see it. First, you can only go where the river goes, and second, while you begin on a lively stream meandering through scenic canyons, that stream will gradually and inevitably widen and flatten until, finally, regrettably, it has become a muddy elongated bathtub. It really ought to be the other way around.

Seen from the air, most rivers look like snakes, and as you paddle around each curve, the view ahead changes very slowly as the distant mountains on one side gradually emerge from behind a screen of intervening ridges just as the distant mountains on the other side are gradually obscured. The mountains along the Wind River were workmanlike and honest, but they were hardly majestic, and we paddled through them in less than a week. For the rest of the trip, we passed through essentially flat terrain, hunkered down between cut banks that blocked our view on either side. Occasionally, briefly, we'd see a black bear scrambling up the bank or a moose clomping through the shallows of a tributary creek, but for days the afternoons in particular were an endless, stupefying succession of stroke after stroke after stroke. In the end, canoeing the Wind required considerable effort to be weighed against rewards that were hard to define.

Participants on guided trips to remote places like the Wind River often trade stories about other trips they've taken, and so Dorothy, a rumpled, grandmotherly sort from Victoria, BC, told me about a canoe trip she'd taken on a Barrens river 800 miles to the east. I immediately asked her about mosquitoes. Not bad, she said, which I interpreted to mean that there hadn't been enough to pick her up and carry her away. But she praised the river and the guides and the food, so I sent for a brochure and found that the company in question, Black Feather, led trips on rivers all across Canada, including several in the Mackenzie Mountains. One of the trips was on the Mountain River. I made a phone call. *Does this river stay in the mountains where it belongs, I asked? Are the mountains picturesque? Does it rain much?* "It's a great trip," they said.

The Mountain River was a big step up from the Wind, funneling through five canyons before joining the Mackenzie, the biggest river in Canada. We'd be paddling through dozens of rapids and many sets of standing waves, so our canoes were fitted with spray decks, canvas covers that kept the boats and paddlers dry. The spray decks were bright orange, with two cockpits. I used them as foreground in many photographs.

I looked forward to bouncing through each set of rapids we encountered, to feeling the power of the river beneath us. I occasionally responded too slowly to the guide's commands, so that we swung around and ran through a rapid backwards, but I had faith in his ability to keep us right side up, and suspected that he enjoyed thwarting the small mishaps I invited.

Each day after we beached the canoes and set up camp, I had ample time to hike to a vantage point or traipse along the shore with my camera and tripod. I hadn't thought to take a camera to Finland—I didn't own one at the time—and I'd seen images every day that begged to be recorded. I did take a camera and thirty rolls of film to Nepal, and friends enjoyed the resulting slide show, especially those who saw it after I'd edited it down to a single carousel. Slide shows of my wilderness trips became a tradition that transported my friends as close as they cared to go places they would always regard as cold and uncomfortable.

The slides documented memories, but I was after more than that. I wanted to take photographs that conveyed the spare beauty and the stillness of the North, images with the assured composition and rich, even light I saw in coffee table books by popular landscape photographers. And often there was such light—golden light on riverside cliffs, gorgeous light on clouds clearing after a squall, soft light on smooth granite boulders. I did my best to capture it on film.

The Mountain River was equal to its name, but it too finally slowed and thickened to a mocha slurry. We paddled for two days on the broad, featureless Mackenzie and pulled out at a native community where we pitched our tents on the dock. Our last night's lullaby was the howling of chained sled dogs.

I wanted more. When I could afford it, I signed up for a trip on the Natla-Keele, which was the next river system south of the Mountain. It was an exploratory trip, so we would be adventurers in a tiny sense, although Wendy, the lead guide, had seen the river from the air and studied it carefully on topographic maps. The Natla-Keele was Skill Level 3—the Mountain River tilted so that it was steeper and faster—and the first sixty miles were a more or less continuous series of rapids, a *rock garden* as the guides would say. We scouted many of these rapids before we ran them, which was prudent, but I sometimes felt as if we were stopping a roller coaster at the top of every rise to tighten the bolts.

We had a fair amount of weather on the Natla-Keele, which gave the trip a sort of damp authenticity. Each dollop of chill and bluster made me feel less like a tenderfoot who visited the North only in summer, knowing that for most of the year the river would be frozen and the land white and still. When it rained while we were in camp, we rigged a large tarp and gathered beneath it, stoking the fire, drying our socks and playing Hearts while tributary creeks rose in a froth and snow dusted the higher ridges around us. I got to know the paddlers who had been relaxing in camp while I was out wandering with my camera. And that delicious sense of security that comes from being home on a stormy night intensified as I lay in my sleeping bag with rain smacking the tent a few inches above my face.

Having canoed the Natla-Keele, I concluded that the rest of Canada's northern rivers were either too flat, too buggy or too frequently visited, and I was open to suggestion. Wendy suggested sea kayaking on the southeast coast of Greenland. I'd never been in a kayak—or to Greenland—but flat-water paddling sounded benign, and the trip would be farther north, closer to twenty-four hour daylight and the Pole. The waters offshore could be a puzzle of fractured floe ice, and there were icebergs. Icebergs closed the deal.

I'd flown over Greenland on the way to Finland. At cruising altitude, it had no discernible features save the occasional dark peak poking through the ice cap. Now, it seemed barely less austere as we approached at 8,000 feet from Iceland. I saw nothing but rock and ice, and I remembered a snide comment from one of my coworkers. *Just once*, he'd said, *I think you should take a vacation in a place with tables and chairs and a wine list.* In fact, there was a restaurant with linen tablecloths in the hamlet of Angmagssalik. They served roasted seal meat that tasted like pork marinated in tuna fish oil, but for that we'd have to wait until the last day of our trip.

We spent our first two days in the small village of Kulusuk, assembling and packing the two-person folding Klepper kayaks, and waiting for the wind to blow the ice offshore so we could begin paddling. The houses in the village were painted the brick red and mustard of a Danish farming community, but little else about the place was charming. The roads and yards, concealed by snow most of the year, were strewn with beer bottles and stale dog shit. Villagers butchered seals straight from their boats and left the flippers and strands of offal scattered across the beach. The kids were curious and friendly, but alcoholism was an ongoing problem. At three in the morning, a drunk wandered into the cottage where we were sleeping to ask for a light. We were relieved to get on the water.

While I concluded in the end that paddling a kayak was more efficient and more elegant than paddling a canoe, it took me a long time to figure out the basics— pushing the blades more than pulling them, describing a sort of continuous figure eight with my wrists, and sliding the blades out of the freezing water at the right angle so they didn't drip on my forearms with every stroke. I shared a kayak with Wendy, who was a powerful paddler, but we brought up the rear for a week until I became marginally competent.

Rivers don't have tides, but fiords do. If we didn't stop for the day close to high tide, we'd have to lug the fully laden boats over slippery rocks to stow them above the tide line. Wind could pack ice against the shore and cut us off from open water, or it could build up hazardous waves while we were committed to an open crossing. Guides thought about these things all the time. I simply awaited instructions.

We were well north of the tree line, and what little vegetation there was hugged the ground below raw mountains streaked with glaciers. Animals were scarce. The seals were understandably cagey about being hunted, but we saw no land mammals at all and only a half dozen species of bird. What made Greenland compelling to me, apart from the steep mountains, narrow fiords and rich light, was the ice. We paddled past occasional icebergs, some drifting with the tide and others grounded in shallow water, some modest in size and some enormous, especially when seen from a kayak. An iceberg is continually being eaten away at the water line by waves and wind, and eventually it becomes top heavy. Then it slowly tips over to one side or another and ponderously rocks back and forth until it finds its new center of gravity. As a result of all this erosion and toppling, each iceberg has a complex, unique shape.

The floe ice—the maze of last winter's fractured sea ice—made navigation interesting as we threaded our way through it. The fractured pieces looked thick and substantial, although wave action was eroding them, too. The underwater shelves formed by this erosion, some so wide and deep that we could paddle over them, were the translucent turquoise of a tropical lagoon in water close to freezing.

From a vantage point ashore, these same sheets of ice looked thin and fragile. They moved so slowly with the tide that you had to watch carefully to be certain they were moving at all. It's an essential experience of Arctic summer to sit in the soft light of evening and watch the drifting ice, gazing out over the same fiord where, earlier in the day, you'd looked at the shoreline as you paddled laboriously for the better part of the afternoon. You would think nowhere else on earth could be so profoundly quiet, and then a slab of ice would suddenly split in half with the *whoomph!* of distant artillery. And then the silence resumed.

Steve, a seasoned Northern guide, likes to tell clients about the time he showed his family slides from his early trips along the shores of Ellesmere Island. Slides, no doubt, of tidewater glaciers oozing down to a fiord sprinkled with ice. *Oh, my,* said his mother. *It looks a lot like the Arctic.* And so it did. But Ellesmere didn't seem especially like Greenland, at least to me. As we paddled along its coast, we saw little ice, but we shared the fiords with a whole community of animals. Narwhals broke the surface of the water offshore from one of our campsites. Bearded seals popped up near the kayaks. A polar bear stood upright on floe ice a couple hundred yards away. But the most prevalent creatures were walruses. They swam past us, singly or in small groups, spraying water as they exhaled, looking just a little like hippopotamuses on the Zambezi. They snoozed on the ice in plump clumps, occasionally scratching themselves with flippers like clowns' feet. Their cries—low, moaning barks—carried for miles over flat water, as distinctive as the call of a loon or the song of a Canyon Wren on the Colorado River.

Land mammals are less common on Ellesmere because there's less to eat on land than there is in the water, but there are Arctic foxes and hares and the wonderfully ponderous muskox. I set out after dinner one evening with another kayaker to see if we could find the source of the fresh droppings and hoof prints behind our campsite. Brian and I skirted the edge of a glacier and headed up a steep ridge. We crested one rise after another, finding more pellets and hoof prints, but no muskox. After well more than an hour, we were getting close to the rocky skyline. *Why,* we wondered, *would a foraging animal climb so high?* We hiked up over one more knoll and—voila—there she was, fifty feet away. She stared at us and snorted, rubbing her head against a front leg. *Don't worry*, said Brian, who had seen musk-oxen before. *She's just getting ready to charge.* This seemed improbable on the steep, rock-strewn slope, but I hunkered down behind a boulder anyway while Brian edged closer with his camera.

To look at a wild animal and say, in effect, *Aw, gee* is to be seduced by furriness into ignoring the harshness of its life. I was seduced. The muskox's impassive eyes were the size and color of chocolate truffles. Each time she took a step, her stately movements were amplified by the lavish coat of guard hairs that hung swaying from her flanks like upside down prairie grass. Brian and I kept her company for half an hour while she grazed. Then we hiked to the top of the ridge, had a look around, and walked quietly into camp at three in the morning.

At seventy-eight degrees north latitude in July, the light at midnight is not greatly different from the light at noon—subdued, but not dusky. The lack of customary days and nights and the absence of familiar daily rituals dampen awareness of time. Even in Greenland, jets on polar routes flew overhead and local villagers motored back and forth in open boats. But Grise Fiord, the only community on Ellesmere Island, was two hundred miles away. The Inuit haven't lived or hunted around the group of fiords we're exploring for many years. Many of their stone artifacts—low dwelling walls, fox traps, burial mounds and simple kayak stands—have stood untouched, except by archeologists, for centuries. What happens on Ellesmere is that muskoxen graze, birds migrate, ice forms and melts, and time passes unmeasured.

On our last full day on the island, after we had cleared the boulders from a stretch of flat river bar where a Twin Otter would land the next morning to pick us up, four of us hiked inland, following the course of a glacial stream up to a rolling plateau. We saw two muskoxen—small, dark blobs—and approached them slowly. The closest was another female. She clambered straight toward us, then veered to the side and stood expectantly as if to say *What next?* After a moment, she headed off to join the other muskox, a male, farther out on the plain. The wind had picked up, driving small pellets of snow through the nippy air. Like my companions, I wanted to continue walking across this wonderfully bleak landscape where we could credibly imagine that no one else had set foot for centuries. I wanted to get a sense of the winter that would soon settle over the land, to push off the moment when we would stuff our wallets back into our pockets and check to make sure we had our tickets for our flights home. But in our hearts that moment had already arrived. We turned around so we'd be back to camp in time for dinner.

9 781732 774759